שמחת בת מצוה

BAT MITZVAH CELEBRATION

לורן ברכה

LAUREN BELLE

פרשת יתרו

FEBRUARY 10, 2007

PARSHAT YITRO

The Jewish Woman's
Book of Wisdom

The Jewish Woman's Book of Wisdom

Thoughts From Prominent Jewish
Women on Spirituality,
Identity, Sisterhood,
Family, and Faith

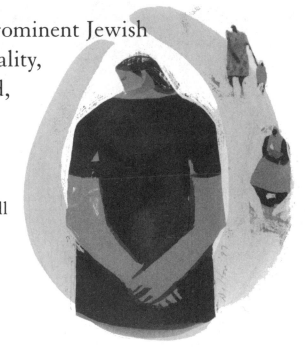

EDITED BY Ellen Jaffe-Gill

CITADEL PRESS
Kensington Publishing Corp.
www.kensingtonbooks.com

CITADEL PRESS books are published by

Kensington Publishing Corp.
850 Third Avenue
New York, NY 10022

All Kensington titles, imprints, and distributed lines are available at special quantity discounts for bulk purchases for sales promotions, premiums, fund raising, educational, or institutional use. Special book excerpts or customized printings can also be created to fit specific needs. For details, write or phone the office of the Kensington special sales manager: Kensington Publishing Corp., 850 Third Avenue, New York, NY 10022, attn: Special Sales Department, phone 1-800-221-2647.

Kensington and the K logo Reg. U.S. Pat. & TM Office
Citadel Press is a trademark of Kensington Publishing Corp.

First printing 1998

10 9 8 7 6 5

Printed in the United States of America

Library of Congress Cataloging-in-Publication Data

The Jewish woman's book of wisdom : thoughts from prominent Jewish
   women on spirituality, identity, sisterhood, family, and faith /
   edited by Ellen Jaffe-Gill.
      p.   cm.
   ISBN 1-55972-480-3 (hc.)
   1. Women in Judaism.   2. Jewish women—United States—Religious
life.   3. Feminism—Religious aspects—Judaism.   4. Jewish
meditations.   5. Judaism—United States.   I. Jaffe-Gill, Ellen.
BM729.W6J47   1998
296′.082—dc21   98–25600
                                                              CIP

For Spencer,
whose wisdom never fails me,
and in memory of Bella Abzug,
a wise woman
who kept the faith

Contents

Editor's Preface

PUTTING TOGETHER a book called *The Jewish Woman's Book of Wisdom* should have been about as challenging as compiling *The NBA Forward's Book of Height*. After all, Jewish women historically have had a reputation for *sechel,* a Yiddish term that translates most often to "common sense" but also includes large dollops of logic and insight. And, in whatever society they live, contemporary Jewish women tend to pursue education and post achievements well out of proportion to their numbers in the community, reinforcing an image as both thinkers and doers.

Though I wasn't looking for challenge in this project, challenge found me soon enough. My task quickly became a matter of sorting through not enough on the one hand and much too much on the other. I wanted to include as much historical material as possible to give an idea of Jewish women's wisdom through the centuries, and I found references to many women whose words I'm sure would have enriched these pages—had I been able to find them.

Where are the Torah commentaries of Beruriah, a scholar who lived in the second century C.E., whose voice is captured in just a few snippets of the Talmud and whose erudition so threatened the rabbis that they reportedly drove her to suicide? Where are the writings of Licoricia of Winchester, a Jewish woman admired throughout medieval England for her business acumen? Where are the letters of Gracia Nasí, who rescued many Jews from the tentacles of the Inquisition after extricating herself? After reading a magazine article about Chana Rochel, a respected expositor of Torah in early nineteenth-century Poland, I e-mailed the author: Where could I find her actual teachings? His reply came back quickly: "Gee, I don't know . . ."

That was the sad discovery—that so many voices of wise Jewish women have been silenced by failure to record their words or keep the scraps of paper on which they wrote, or, in some accounts, by the attribution to men of what they said and wrote. Perhaps a sense that this silencing must never again be permitted is one reason contemporary Jewish women have been so prolific in their writing, so driven to make their voices heard.

In choosing from the writings of Jewish women during this century, my challenge became one of overabundance rather than scarcity, especially since the contemporary women's movement has given women both a more vigorous voice and a larger forum. How to select from the hundreds of writings that represent the flowering of Jewish women's scholarship, insight, and experience?

One way was to choose writings of women for whom Jewishness was more than an accident of birth, who maintained a conscious relationship with Jewishness as ethnicity, Judaism as religious faith, or both. If there is an emphasis in this volume on matters of faith and spirituality, it's because much of Jewish women's wisdom seems to be rooted in our relationships with family, the cycle of life, and our communities, all of which lead back to the teachings of Judaism. Then too, many contemporary Jewish women have discovered their voices in the structures of communal Jewish life, as rabbis, cantors, educators, scholars.

This focus still provided a wealth of material that included the myriad crosscurrents and contradictions informing Jewish women's relationships to God, Jewish ritual, and Jewish identity. There's the question of faith itself: Many contemporary adults see having, let alone expressing, religious faith as a surrender of reason and autonomy, as childish and subservient. But here, at the end of the twentieth century, we live in a time of spiritual search, when many adults who never gave religion a thought are looking for answers beyond the material world. There's the exasperation with traditional Judaism's patriarchal character that has caused thousands of Jewish women to check out of Jewish life, while at the same time, women as never before are claiming Judaism for themselves, both in traditional and liberal circles. As clergy and as laypersons, Jewish women have created prayers, rituals, and ceremonies that reflect the milestones of their lives, give them a voice in the congregation, and place them unmistakably alongside the men at Sinai. Today, there are very few Jewish women who cannot find a niche for themselves within Judaism as a faith community. The struggle to find that place and the fruits of that struggle are reflected in this volume.

What started for me as a simple job of work became not only a challenge but a community. How could I not become emotionally invested in the writings of people who, after all, are my sisters? I grieve for the women missing from these pages because their voices were silenced by hostility and neglect. I grieve for those present in these pages whose voices were silenced by oppressors. I reach out to those women who wrote in pain and in fear, applaud those who helped make a better world for us all, rejoice with those who found their way to renewed connection and faith.

I am blessed by the fact that in just a few months' time, I learned from a hundred teachers, and feel privileged to be part of one of the most powerful forces in Jewish life today, *kol isha:* a woman's voice.

Acknowledgments

No BOOK IS CREATED in isolation, and putting together *The Jewish Woman's Book of Wisdom* permitted me to form many new connections with women of scholarship and eloquence. Thanks are due to my editor at Carol Publishing, Carrie Cantor; my literary agent, Barbara Markowitz; and to the dozens of people who responded to my requests for writings, permissions, and artwork. My special gratitude goes to Ellen Frankel, Ellen Umansky, Letty Cottin Pogrebin, and Cynthia Ozick, who were especially generous with their words, insights, and Rolodexes.

I could not have finished this book on deadline were it not for United Teachers Los Angeles, the union to which I belonged for fourteen years, and my boss there, Steve Blazak. They arranged for me to leave my classroom and help put out the union's newspaper just when I needed a day job that took forty hours of my time each week, not sixty. And I could not have done this work without the constant support of my husband, Spencer Gill, who trusts me more than I trust myself to get a job done and do it well. I am grateful for his love and wisdom every day.

1

A Woman's Voice
FEMININE SPIRITUALITY

I'm Weary of Mountains

SANDY EISENBERG SASSO

Must we always go up to some
mountain
with Abraham, with Isaac to Moriah?
The air is so thin up there,
and it's hard to breathe.

Must we always go up to some
mountain
with Moses to Sinai?
It's so far from the earth,
and what's below appears so small
You can forget it's real.

Must we always go up to some
mountain
with Moses to Nebo?
Climbing—there's only one way
and loneliness.

Must we always go up to some
mountain

From "A Pilgrimage Prayer," first published in "Introduction: Unwrapping the Gift," *Women and Religious Ritual,* ed. Lesley A. Northrup (Pastoral Press, 1993).

with Elijah to Carmel?
The ascent is not hard.
It's the descending—
too easy to slip
with no one to catch your fall.

I'm weary of mountains
where we're always looking up
or looking down and sacrificing
so our neck hurts
and we need glasses.
Our feet upon the mountains
are blistered,
and our shoes are always wrong—
Not enough "sole."

Can we sit with Sarah in a tent,
next to Deborah under a palm tree,
with Hannah in prayer
alongside Miriam by the sea—
to wash our feet,
to catch our breath and
our soul?

SANDY EISENBERG SASSO (born 1947), who has written many liturgical poems, is
co-rabbi of Congregation Beth El Zedeck in Indianapolis, Indiana.

I Rejoice in the God-light

Minnie D. Louis

I am no pessimist; I rejoice in the God-light that floods the world, and ever more and more beautifies it to my spiritual vision . . . I would have this light focused on every soul, glorifying it like the Rembrandt light on a picture. But it seems to me that this light can only be converged through the spirituality of the intellect and the intelligence of the spirituality. . . .

Do we not try to cage our God today? Do not our priests devote their lives to guarding Him in walls of porphyry and onyx and every costly adjunct? And will He remain there? Already from cathedral, minster, temple, abbey, there and there, the life has long since fled; many of them are mere mausoleums for both the living and the dead. . . . But, oh! women, it is we with our "sanative conscience" that must turn in the full, strong light, and make chancel, aisle and transept, lectern and pew, glow in the sunbeams of a new spirituality.

Minnie D. Louis (1841–1922), a founding member of the National Council of Jewish Women, made these remarks in a 1895 speech to the NJCW.

From "The Influence of Women in Bringing Religious Conviction to Bear upon Daily Life," *American Hebrew* (28 June 1895).

God Must Be Dug Out

Etty Hillesum

Etty Hillesum (1914–1943) was a twenty-seven-year-old psychology student in Amsterdam when she began keeping a diary in March 1941. The journal chronicles the life of a young woman who could just as easily have lived today as them, a twentysomething who lived in a house with other young people, had affairs, didn't think much about religion. But Hillesum was also a witness to the rising terror of the Holocaust, which carried her to Westerbork detention camp in August 1943 and to Auschwitz in September 1943. She died there, six weeks short of her thirtieth birthday. Her diary and her letters from Westerbork survived.

At the time of this diary entry, 8 June 1941, Hillesum was still more concerned with her romantic and spiritual life than with the Nazis, who had occupied Holland the previous year.

I think . . . I'll "turn inwards" for half an hour each morning before work, and listen to my inner voice. Lose myself. You could also call it meditation. I am still a bit wary of that word. But anyway, why not? . . .

But it's not so simple, that sort of "quiet hour." It has to be learnt. A lot of unimportant inner litter and bits and pieces have to be swept out first. . . . So let this be the aim of the meditation: to turn one's innermost being into a vast empty plain, with none of that treacherous undergrowth to impede the view. So that something of "God" can enter you, and something of "Love" too. Not the kind of love-de-luxe that you revel in deliciously for half an

From *An Interrupted Life: The Diaries of Etty Hillesum, 1941–1943,* trans. Arno Pomerans (Pantheon Books, 1983).

hour, taking pride in how sublime you can feel, but the love you can apply to small, everyday things.

I might of course read the Bible each morning, but I don't think I'm ready for that. I still worry about the real meaning of the book, rather than lose myself in it.

By 26 August 1941, Hillesum seems to have made some progress in meditation.

There is a really deep well inside me. And in it dwells God. Sometimes I am there too. But more often stones and grit block the well, and God is buried beneath. Then He must be dug out again.

I imagine that there are people who pray with their eyes turned heavenwards. They seek God outside themselves. And there are those who bow their head and bury it in their hands. I think that these seek God inside.

To Replace Those They Had Lost

Shoshanna Gershenzon

The very characteristics and behaviors which, according to recent studies, may have helped women to survive in extreme circumstances [such as the Holocaust]—their habits of caring, caretaking, and concern for others, their ability to exploit limited resources, their emphasis on cooperative and consensus behavior—not only contributed to survival, but led many to create and maintain ad hoc "families" to replace those they had lost. These same characteristics and behaviors, applied by feminists to the Divine Feminine, may help us, as women, to reconnect with a Creator who has lost so much of Creation.

God, like us, seeks connection with Her creatures, both those who inflict suffering and those who bear it. The corollary to reaffirming the mothering and caretaking aspects of the Divine is acknowledging the unbreakable connection between Creator and creature and accepting the pain and joy of inhabiting our Mother's universe.

Shoshanna Gershenzon (born 1929) is a retired professor of Jewish studies, most recently at California State University, Northridge. She has published numerous articles on medieval Jewish history.

Pulling the Pendulum Back

LAURA GELLER

Creating new rituals that celebrate women's experience is only the beginning of the "tikkun" [healing] that can overcome women's marginality and unlock spirituality. There are other dimensions of women's experience that point to a feminist theology, a different way of speaking about God that emerges from a different experience of God. . . .

Translated into theological terms, women's experience of God may be more an experience of immanence than one of transcendence, the God we experience within and among us as opposed to the God over and against us. There has always been a dialectic tension in Judaism between transcendence and immanence. In Rabbinic Judaism the pendulum swung well over to the side of transcendence; feminist Judaism is pulling the pendulum back. We need to explore these different images of God in our tradition—the image in the midrash of God as a nursing mother with Torah the milk she gives her child Israel, the image of the Shechinah, the God who is the source of [r]achamim, womb-like compassion, the God Jacob/Israel saw in the face of his brother.

But we cannot stop there; we must find ways to translate them into our prayer. Our liturgy was created by men; it emphasizes those images of God and community that reflected the values of the men who framed it. A new liturgy must be accessible to women as well as men, drawing on all of our experiences of God and community.

From "Symposium: What Kind of Tikkun?" *Tikkun,* vol. 1 (1), 1986.

In 1994, Laura Geller (born 1950), the third woman ordained through the Reform movement, became the first woman appointed as the spiritual leader of a large congregation, Temple Emanuel in Beverly Hills, California, now numbering more than a thousand members.

Friday Afternoon: The Rabbi's Wife

Enid Shomer

Inside the yeshiva
he's busy naming things
while I, like Eve,
watch the smallest
movements of the world—
grass bending
as if it aches,
a bird that carries
lust in its beak.

Through the window
I've seen him
bent over the text,
saliva flying from his mouth
as he reads and debates,
reads and debates,
the morning kiss
of the phylactery
still faintly visible
on his forehead.

"Friday Afternoon: The Rabbi's Wife," in *Stalking the Florida Panther* (Word Works, 1987).

Though he's nourished
by the play of words
and feels the heat
of flame-tipped
letters, at sundown
when he seeks the Sabbath
Bride, it is I who serve
the steaming food, I
who inhale the pungent fume
as the matchtip wakes
the candle and I set
the fire free.

Enid Shomer (born 1944) is a prize-winning poet and fiction writer, author of four books. Her work appears in *The New Yorker, Atlantic Monthly, Poetry, Paris Review, Tikkun, Midstream,* and other magazines. Her books include *Imaginary Men,* a collection of short stories.

Covenant

SHARON KESSLER

In the desert
where old legends
conspire, we
are making fresh
tracks in the sand,
carrying our burden
to some resting place.

        Above
the black crest
of rock,
an arc of slow fire
rises. Morning again.
We march forward,
a tribe of mute warriors,
daughters of a race
so lost
no legend tells of us.

Published in *Tikkun,* July/August 1989.

We too heard voices in the wilderness
but we built
no tabernacle
to contain them.

The sign of the covenant
is not incised upon our flesh,

but deep in the one heart
of our body
the everlasting bush burns
and is not consumed.

Sharon Kessler (born 1957) was raised in New York and has lived in Israel since 1981. Her poems have been published in various journals and anthologies in the United States and Israel, and she is the author of a chapbook of poems, *The Insistence of Names*.

Whenever We Faltered, She Was There

LAURA METZGER

LAURA METZGER (born 1950), director of outreach for Congregation Adath Jeshurun in Louisville, Kentucky, conceived a eulogy for Miriam, Moses' sister, as a midrash, a story that fills in the gaps in Torah.

9 Iyyar 2487

Our Miryam is gone. We, the daughters of Israel, sob like babies when mother is out of sight. . . . Without you, we would still be in Egypt, nameless, less than slaves, the wives and daughters of slaves. With you, we have been proud women, the support of our families, the conscience of our people. . . .

It was Miryam who told us what to take: cloaks and robes, cloth and fibre, kneading bowls, cooking vessels, stirring sticks and jugs. . . . As for food and drink, take only what you need for today and tomorrow, she advised. God will provide for us.

Across the Reed Sea, and safe from Egyptian warriors, as soon as Moses finished his song of success, Miryam took timbrel in hand and led the women in dance.

Whenever we faltered, she was there to encourage. When the journey grew difficult, and the men railed at Moses and Aaron, we took our woes to Miryam. Heeding, knowing our fears, she comforted us. She was always there to wrap a cloak around a child shivering with fright, stroke the brow of a woman in labor. Miryam turned our eyes away from idolatry, held us close under the protecting wings of our God. . . .

From "Eulogy for Our Mother Miryam," *CCAR Journal,* Summer 1997.

Oh, our mother Miryam, how we miss you. Your death came so suddenly, we had no time to prepare. You did not pass on your cloak to another to make a bed for a child or to wrap around the shoulders of a tired laborer. You did not pass on your stirring stick or your kneading bowl to feed orphans and those too old to cook. You did not pass on your timbrel. Only the memory of your voice remains.

And who will carry on? All of us, as you taught us, Mother Miryam. All of us.

Every woman has arms to carry and to hug. Every woman has hands to build and to cook, to craft and to shape. Every woman has ears to hear the needs and worries, fears and hopes of the people. Eyes to see the past and envision the future. Voices to lift in song, feet to dance in celebration. We are the inheritors of your gift, beloved Miryam. We the daughters of Israel.

We All Stood Together

MERLE FELD

For Rachel Adler

My brother and I were at Sinai
He kept a journal
of what he saw
of what he heard
of what it all meant to him

I wish I had such a record
of what happened to me there

It seems like every time I want to write
I can't
I'm always holding a baby
one of my own
or one for a friend
always holding a baby
so my hands are never free
to write things down

To be published in *A Spiritual Life* (SUNY Press, forthcoming).

And then
as time passes
the particulars
the hard data
the who what when where why
slip away from me
and all I'm left with is
the feeling

But feelings are just sounds
the vowel barking of a mute

My brother is so sure of what he heard
after all he's got a record of it
consonant after consonant after consonant

If we remembered it together
we could recreate holy time
sparks flying

MERLE FELD (born 1947) has written numerous poems that express her Jewish self, including several that turn up frequently in liberal prayerbooks. Her latest collection is *A Spiritual Life,* to be published in 1999.

2

The Struggle

RECONCILING JUDAISM AND FEMINISM

A Little on the Margins

SUSANNAH HESCHEL

Being a feminist—and I feel as though I was born a feminist!—gives me a different perspective. When I was a teenager, I used to argue with my parents' friends who taught at the Jewish Theological Seminary about women's participation in synagogue services. They said that a woman on the *bimah* would be distracting to men and that if women were counted in the *minyan,* men wouldn't come to synagogue any more. They quoted the Talmud, which prohibits women from reading from the Torah for the sake of the "honor of the congregation." I began to realize that the entire Jewish system is constructed as if the congregation were exclusively a congregation of men. What about women's honor, our religiosity, our spiritual needs and experiences? More and more I came to see that the issue of women in Judaism was not simple, and effecting change wouldn't come from modifying this or that point of Jewish law. Instead, I saw that the entire system excluded women's perspective. . . .

Yet, I am still drawn to the Judaism that my father [the great scholar, author, and activist Abraham Joshua Heschel] defined in his books and my parents created in our home. This is not the rigid arbitrary religion I encountered in the yeshiva, nor as sexist and exclusivist as some feminist critics have portrayed it. I want to remain a committed Jew and a feminist, even though being both has often left me feeling tremendous pain and anger. . . .

From "Contradictions," in *The Invisible Thread,* by Diana Bletter and Lori Grinker (The Jewish Publication Society, 1989).

My beliefs have put me in an interesting position—a little on the margins of both Judaism and feminism, always looking at things from other perspectives, always seeing tensions and ambiguities. My father used to say, "Show me a person who has no problems and I'll show you a fool." Too many Jews today want to solve everything, find simple solutions and answers—as if all we have are simple questions—when actually we have profound and exciting problems. I like the struggle and the conflicts. I don't want to live in a fool's paradise.

SUSANNAH HESCHEL is the editor of *On Being a Jewish Feminist* and a volume of her father's work, *Moral Grandeur and Spiritual Audacity: Essays,* and she is the author of the recent book *Abraham Geiger and the Jewish Jesus.*

We Weren't Friends or Comrades

Vivian Gornick

When was the first time I saw it? Which movie was it? I can't remember. I remember only that at one of them, in the early seventies, I suddenly found myself listening to the audience laugh hysterically while [Woody] Allen made a dreadful fool of the girl on the screen, and I realized that he had to make a fool of her, that he would always have to make a fool of her, because she was the foil: the instrument of his unholy deprivation, the exasperating source of life's mean indifference. I said to myself, "This is dis-*gust*-ting," and as I said it I knew I'd been feeling this way all my life: from Milton Berle to Saul Bellow to Woody Allen. I had always laughed, but deep inside I'd frozen up, and now I saw why.

Milton Berle with his mother-in-law jokes, Saul Bellow with the mistresses who hold out and the wives who do him in, Mel Brooks and Woody Allen with the girl always and only the carrot at the end of the stick. Every last one of them was trashing women. Using women to savage the withholding world. Using us. Their mothers, their sisters, their wives. To them, we weren't friends or comrades. We weren't even Jews or gentiles. We were just girls.

At that moment I knew that I would never again feel myself more of a Jew than a woman. I had never suffered as men did for being a Jew in a Christian world because, as a Jew, I had not known that I wanted the world. Now, as a woman, I knew I wanted the world and I suffered.

Vivian Gornick (born 1935) is a feminist writer and author of the books *Fierce Attachments* and *The End of the Novel of Love*.

From "Twice an Outsider: On Being Jewish and a Woman," *Tikkun,* March/April 1989.

Our Religious Duty to Dismantle Patriarchy

Tikva Frymer-Kensky

The Halakha, with its many emendations, interpreters, collectors, codifiers, judges, and commentators is sometimes referred to by the image of *yam ha-halakha,* the sea of Halakha. But a sea is large, and overwhelming, and allows people to flounder and get lost or drown. The proliferation of interpretation brings us to ever deeper waters, but we may lose sight of the other side. Halakha is more like a river, wide and deep, that is flowing between our past and our goal. When it meanders too much or gets wild or destructive, it is our job to keep it flowing toward the divine order, *malkhut shamayim.* We have the tools to direct and refine the Halakha, for the halakhic system has given us ample instruction of the ways to change, divert, abrogate, and amend our rules. . . .

To deny people's full humanity is to remove them from divinity, and if we lessen the divine image of anyone, we diminish it in all of us. . . . If we say a woman cannot testify, what do we say about her? If a woman is anchored to someone (who has not given her a divorce), have we subordinated her humanity to his?

Ancient Israel could not foresee everything. The Bible never transformed its own social structure. It doesn't abolish slavery, possibly because the biblical socio-economic system was not capable of surviving without slavery. When the Rabbis came to the decision that slavery was wrong, they abolished it. The domination of one person over another can never lead to God.

From "Toward a Liberal Theory of Halakha," *Tikkun,* July/August 1995.

Patriarchy is another form of domination, by males over females. Now that we have come to this realization, it is our religious duty to dismantle patriarchy. . . . When we examine Halakha according to our best ethical understanding, we are not evaluating Torah by secular values. Our ethical principles are also a part of Torah.

TIKVA FRYMER-KENSKY is a professor of Jewish studies at the University of Chicago. Her books include *In the Wake of the Goddesses: Women Culture and the Biblical Transformation of Pagan Myth; Motherprayer;* and *Victims, Virgins, and Victors: A New Reading of Women of the Bible.*

Judaism Will Emerge Stronger

Blu Greenberg

For me, at least, the process is not over, this interweaving of feminism and Judaism. Because one is continuously exposed to those encounters and incidents that affect one's worldview, I suspect I will have ample occasion to go through several more cycles of thought and feeling before it all stabilizes. I intend to keep my eyes wide open, watching to see what works and what doesn't. . . .

Two things I know for sure. My questioning will never lead me to abandon tradition. I am part of a chain that is too strong to break, and though it needs no protection from me, a child of the tradition, I want to protect it with the fierceness of a mother protecting her young. But I also know that I never can yield the new value of women's equality, even though it may conflict with Jewish tradition. To do so would be to affirm the principle of a hierarchy of male and female, and this I no longer believe to be an axiom of Judaism.

I feel instinctively that drawing the lines is important and correct at both fundamental and transcendental levels. Divisions of labor and function are, in fact, humanly expedient; there is a remarkable staying power of sexual identity and distinctiveness, the uniqueness of male and female beyond biology. Yet there are many instances in which the sex-role divisions in Judaism do not work. To deny participation in this or that experience because one is

From "A Yeshiva Girl Among the Feminists," in *On Women and Judaism* (The Jewish Publication Society, 1981).

a man or a woman is an act of inhumanity. Somehow, Judaism will have to find a way to bridge the gap.

Meanwhile, there is probably a great deal of tension in store for people like me. But that no longer frightens me, neither personally nor in terms of the system. In fact, I suspect—indeed, I know—that ultimately Judaism will emerge stronger and not weaker from this encounter with feminism. Happiness for a mild-mannered yeshiva girl? Less naïveté perhaps, more unrest, a constant probing, endless queries. Surely that's no blueprint for happiness. But the engagement of Judaism and feminism offers something else: new heights to scale, a deeper sense of maturity, and an enlarged scope of responsibility for oneself, society, and the continuity of tradition—exactly what the religious endeavor is all about.

Blu Greenberg (born 1936) has published numerous essays on the roles of women in traditional Judaism.

To Walk With Confidence in the Garden

FRANCINE KLAGSBRUN

In the religious sphere, feminists have delved into women's feelings and experiences as a way of countering patriarchal dominance. Jewishly that has meant rediscovering the feminine aspects of God, of prayer and of the Torah. And that has been a fine, enriching enterprise.

But what concerns me now is that so much importance has been placed on feminine spirituality that we run the danger of defining women's religiosity only in terms of feelings, mysticism, or intuition. We run the risk of stereotyping women as they were stereotyped for centuries as creatures of emotion and instinct while men continue to own the realms of reason and cognition. No. I want women to be learned in law and text as well as to be rich in spirit. I want them to combine spirituality with intellect, to be Rabbi Akiba and to walk with confidence in the garden, having first mastered the more mundane paths of the Torah.

FRANCINE KLAGSBRUN (born 1931) is a writer and lecturer on family, social change, ethics, and feminism. She is the author of *Mixed Feelings: Love, Hate, Rivalry, and Reconciliation Among Brothers and Sisters* and *Jewish Days: A Book of Jewish Life and Culture Around the Year.*

From an untitled column in *Moment,* August 1992.

If Grandma Had Skates

MALKE BINA

Talmud may have been a bit different on certain points if women had been involved. If that would have been the case, I'd enjoy it more and find it more fulfilling. *But it didn't happen.* There's a popular expression in Hebrew that translates as "If Grandma had skates." It means you can't ask What if? It would have been nice if women had also contributed to the Talmud. But it didn't happen. I hate to make an issue of sex. Men were the people who were studying then and for whatever reason women didn't study then. We're dealing with people who had the Jewish nation so much on their minds that they wouldn't go down to sexist issues.

I want every woman to develop to her fullest potential. In the internal way. On the other hand, I'm a practical person and I'm not a radical by any means, and what's going to happen externally I don't know. I don't like to create ruckuses. There's already so much friction and division in the Jewish nation that I don't want to cause any more. There will be many women *able* to write legal opinions, many women who know more what to do in their lives, how to instruct and tell other women. Whether it'll be time to do it or if it will be accepted by society, I don't know. . . .

In order really to be a rabbi of a community and a legal decisor, and to do it properly, you need full concentration, eighteen-hour days devoted to study and community work. I want to have the time to be with my children

From *Words on Fire: One Woman's Journey Into the Sacred* by Vanessa Ochs (Harcourt Brace Jovanovich, 1990).

at meals, have discussions, and talk to my daughter about her ballet. Not that my husband doesn't want that, too, but he removes himself more. We are women. Women can do so many things. But this idea of ultimate power—in the rabbinic sense—and devotion to the community, the way it should be done properly—I think it's something a woman could do if she wished but naturally wouldn't want to.

The Baltimore-born MALKE BINA, a lifelong Orthodox Jew whose name translated from Hebrew means "Queen of Understanding," is a teacher of Talmud to women in Jerusalem.

A Fresh Search for the Hidden Places

Marcia Falk

My own journey as a poet to enact [a] feminist Jewish vision has led me to write new Hebrew *b'rakhot* (blessings) to substitute for the traditional, formulaic ones that have idolized the image of a male lord/God/king ruling over the world. . . . I create and use new images—images such as *eyn ha-khayyim*, "wellspring or source of life," *ma'yan khayyenu*, "fountain or flow of our lives," *nishmat kol khai*, "breath of all living things," and *nitzotzot ha-nefesh*, "sparks of the inner, unseen self"—to serve as fresh metaphors for Divinity. . . . Today I find that every blessing I write journeys toward yet another image of the Divine, and embarks on a fresh search for the hidden places in my life where Divinity may be awakened.

At the same time, the specific language of my images and the structure of my prayers are drawn from traditional Jewish sources, which give historical connection to my labor and, I hope, to the products of my labor. The desire for this connection is deep; being a Jew feels almost as fundamental to my self-definition as being female. Yet it is not just a matter of early-formed identity; I continue, as a feminist, to choose Judaism, despite its problems, because I know that all real relationships entail struggle—and my relationship to Judaism is one through which I continue to grow.

In the end, Judaism's emphasis on unity is a crucial source of awareness for me: it is the foundation of empathy and connectedness; it is the principle that expresses the integrity of existence. As a poet in pursuit of images to

From "Toward a Feminist Jewish Reconstruction of Monotheism," *Tikkun,* July/August 1989.

affirm both diversity and unity, I know that the journey is just—ever—beginning. As a feminist Jew, I hope that if, through community, we support and continue such pursuits, embracing all our truths as parts of a greater whole, we may approach a truly whole and diversified, inclusive and pluralistic vision—and give voice to authentic monotheism.

MARCIA FALK is a noted liturgist and author of *The Book of Blessings*.

The Search for a Separate Woman Self

Jyl Lynn Felman

I am nineteen and do not yet know that I am a lesbian; my hair is very long, past my shoulders. My mother drops me off at Teddy's. Walking into the beauty shop alone for the first time in years, I am light-headed, almost giddy. "Cut it off," I tell a shocked Teddy. "Short." . . . When she's done both of us look directly into the mirror. I'm grinning at my reflection; no more heavy GE blow-dryers or giant orange juice cans, no more hours of preparation, just a quick wash and an easy towel-dry.

I sign the receipt and walk out the door just as my mother drives up to the entranceway and passes me right by. I wait for her to turn around, but she doesn't; she doesn't even recognize me. I wave my hands in the air. My mother backs up the car, looks out the window, and starts screaming. She doesn't say a word, she just screams, over and over again. I'm not sure she'll ever let me back inside the car. We never speak about that moment in the parking lot of Teddy's beauty salon. I don't know exactly what my mother saw in my face once all that thick brown hair was cleared out of the way. I knew that modesty in all things was central to my Jewish mother; so the simple act of cutting off my hair for the hot summer months was ultimately an act of immodesty and thus a permanent embarrassment to her. But at nineteen I had no idea that in cutting my hair short I was also cutting the intense female bonds between us. I had become my own woman, one who thought she could choose for herself how to wear her hair. But I was wrong.

From "L'Dor V Dor: From Generation to Generation," in *Her Face in the Mirror: Jewish Women on Mothers and Daughters,* ed. Faye Moskowitz (Beacon Press, 1994).

Female autonomy, the search for a separate woman self, was never a goal in my family. My mother could not assist her daughters with their—our—sexual development. Any female identity outside of this context was an aberration. So when I knew for sure that I was a lesbian, I was afraid to tell my mother. What I feared most was that I lacked courage, that I would choose a relationship with my beloved mother over a relationship with myself and the woman I had chosen to be my life partner. Twenty years ago there was little in contemporary Jewish theology to assist me in my search for a Jewish feminist lesbian self; at the same time, feminism was rejoicing in the rejection of all things patriarchal, including Judaism and the State of Israel. I felt as though I wandered in the desert alone. Like Lot's wife, I could neither look back, for fear of paralysis, nor go forward on my own sacred journey. I remained caught—as my mother herself was—between two worlds. Only the order had been reversed. While my mother was pulled between her husband and her three daughters, I was pulled between feminism and Judaism—my sisters or my parents.

JYL LYNN FELMAN (born 1954), a professor in the women's studies program at Brandeis University, has written a memoir, *Cravings,* and created the performance piece *I Wish I'd Been Born a Kosher Chicken.*

Dayenu

E. M. BRONER

If Eve had been created in the image of
God
and not as helper to Adam,
it would have sufficed.
Dayenu.

If she had been created as Adam's equal
and not as temptress,
Dayenu.

If she were the first woman to eat
from the Tree of Knowledge,
who brought learning to us,
Dayenu.

If Sarah were recognized as a priestess,
royal in her own lineage,
Dayenu.

If Lot's wife had been honored and not
mocked
when she turned her head

From *The Women's Haggadah,* by E. M. Broner and Naomi Nimrod in *The Telling* (HarperSan-Francisco, 1993).

as devastation befell her children,
and not mocked for the falling
and freezing of her tears,
Dayenu.

If our foremothers had not been
considered
as hardened roots
or fruit-bearing wombs,
but as women in themselves,
Dayenu.

If our fathers had not pitted our mothers
against each other,
like Abraham with Sarah and Hagar
or Jacob with Leah and Rachel
or Elkanah with Hannah and Pnina,
Dayenu.

If Miriam were given her prophet's chair
or the priesthood,
Dayenu.

If the Just Women in Egypt
who caused our redemption
had been given sufficient recognition,
Dayenu.

If women bonding, like Naomi and Ruth,
were the tradition
and not the exception,
Dayenu.

If women were in the Tribal Council and
decided on the laws
that dealt with women,
Dayenu.

If women had also been
the writers of Tanach,
interpreters of our past,
Dayenu.

If women had written the Haggadah
and brought our mothers forth,
Dayenu.

If every generation of women
together with every generation of men
would continue to go out of Egypt,
Dayenu, Dayenu.

E. M. BRONER (born 1927) is the author of ten books, including *A Weave of Women, Ghost Stories,* and *The Telling: The Story of a Group of Jewish Women Who Journey to Spirituality Through Community and Ceremony.*

We Are What We Worship

Kim Chernin

Does Jewish experience rest upon the idea of a single God who is God the Father? That is a fundamental question for Jewish women today. We are what we worship; we become what we are able to imagine. In the name of our God, we give shape to ourselves. . . .

It is a highly radical and subversive act to tell a familiar story in a new way. Once you start to do it you realize that what you call history is another such story and could be told differently, and has been. And then the authoritative tradition starts to crack and crumble. It too, it turns out, is nothing more than a particular selection of various stories, all of which have at one time or another been believed and told. At that point you become far, far less certain how to define the Jewish experience. Perhaps it has been torn with struggle and bloodshed because it is itself filled with self-contradiction and ambivalence, told differently depending on who is telling the story. And perhaps it has been constantly changing, in spite of the study-houses where God the Father was worshiped, where women were excluded, where the text was memorized and passed on, always the same?

It isn't easy to be born to a tradition that must stay the same and simultaneously be constantly changing.

But that's what it means to be Jewish.

And, as my mother always said, why *should* it be easy?

That's what it means to be a Jewish woman, isn't it?

From "In the House of the Flame Bearers," *Tikkun,* May/June 1987.

Kim Chernin (born 1940) is the author of the novel *The Flame Bearers*, the memoir *In My Mother's House*, and other books on Jewish identity and feminism. The above excerpt is from a paper presented at the Women's Studies/Jewish Studies Convergences Conference at Stanford University in 1987.

3

From Generation to Generation

LOVING AND
TEACHING
OUR CHILDREN

Serve God from Your Heart

GLÜCKEL OF HAMELN

The best thing for you, my children, is to serve God from your heart, without falsehood or sham, not giving out to people that you are one thing while, God forbid, in your heart you are another.

Say your prayers with awe and devotion. During the time for prayers, do not stand about and talk of other things. While prayers are being offered to the Creator of the world, hold it a great sin to engage another man in talk about an entirely different matter—shall God Almighty be kept waiting until you have finished your business?

GLÜCKEL OF HAMELN (1646–1724) was a pious North German woman whose memoirs, written over several decades, provide us with a unique window into the way German Jews of the merchant class lived three hundred years ago. The mother of fourteen children, Glückel is often cited as a real-life example of the "woman of valor" celebrated in Proverbs 31.

From *The Memoirs of Glückel of Hameln,* trans. Marvin Lowenthal (Schocken Books, 1977).

The Enemy As Someone to Persuade

CAROL TAVRIS

My mother, Dorothy, may have been deficient in one key requirement of the revolutionary: anger and a corresponding inclination to regard the enemy as uniformly malignant. Instead, my mother regarded the enemy as fodder for persuasion and conversion, which meant that she was prepared to argue from a stance of empathy rather than hostility. Naturally she has encountered ample amounts of sexism and anti-Semitism, but she has handled them as if they were bedbugs in the cot of life: unpleasant but natural forces that were to be eradicated, as best one could, with persistence and pluck.

For example, she once told me about the time she interviewed for a job as a clerk in a law office (a job she needed to support her night school law courses). At the end of the interview, the employer suddenly looked at her and said, "By the way, you aren't Jewish, are you?" "Why yes, I am," said my mother, "but surely that doesn't matter." The interviewer sheepishly admitted that office policy was not to hire Jews. My mother neither accepted this statement passively nor protested it angrily. "Why not?" she said. "Well, um, because Jews are so loud and boisterous," he said.

At that moment the brassy voice of the Irish office manager suddenly rose above the office clatter—cursing a customer. "Oh, I see your problem," said my mother. "You obviously hired one Jewish woman already, and are regretting it." The interviewer laughed. My mother got the job. Eventually she overcame his other major prejudice too, against women lawyers.

From time to time, when I speak of my mother, people ask me three

From "My Mother the Feminist," *Lilith,* Summer 1989.

questions: Doesn't she have any warts? Wasn't there a downside of having a feminist mom? Did you yearn for anything else? Thanks to my mother, I can emphatically understand the reasons for these questions, for our society is so used to blaming mothers for all our ills, and is so skeptical of people who sing only their mothers' praises. So I will answer these questions: Yes, but none as matters. No. No.

All her life my mother has been teaching me wise lessons in word and deed, and now she is showing me how to grow old. For her 80th birthday, my husband and I found two photos of her: one on a horse in the Rockies in 1929, at age 23, and one on a camel in Egypt, taken 50 years later. Now we have a new picture, because my brother's birthday present to her was a ride in a hot-air balloon. "Aren't you nervous about going up in one of those things?" asked a friend the night before the adventure. "I'm not sure," said my mother, "but I have a reputation to uphold."

CAROL TAVRIS (born 1944), the author of *Anger: The Misunderstood Emotion* and *The Mismeasure of Woman,* is a social psychologist living in Los Angeles. Her mother, Dorothy Tavris, is still active in the Brandeis University National Women's Committee and as a counselor for the ACLU at age ninety-two.

Such a Miracle

NAOMI WOLF

[T]he progressive, post-Marxist world of which I was part was profoundly atheistic and hostile to religious and spiritual traditions.... Additionally, some of the hostility to religion from feminists I was around at the time derived from their perception that "God-language" had been so co-opted by the religious right that to use it was to allow oneself to be co-opted.

So it felt embarrassing, a social liability, to admit an interest in God....

But then I gave birth two and a half years ago. That was such a miracle that it's hard not to try to figure out how to address it. The manifest miraculousness of having your child wake up in the morning and look at you! It's hard not to speculate about "where did you come from?" The kind of love that being a parent brings out, that donkey-like, repetitive, abject, egoless love, is closer to a spiritual notion of love than any other kind of love I've experienced.... [T]his kind of experience of love made it easier for me to understand some of what the spiritual traditions were addressing.

NAOMI WOLF (born 1963) is the author of the bestselling *Promiscuities* and *The Beauty Myth*.

From "Starting on My Spiritual Path," *Tikkun,* January/February 1998.

The Highest Goal Is to Imitate God

Lisa Aiken

One of our fundamental obligations as Jews is to imitate God. We were not commanded to become millionaires, professionals, or politicians. We *were* commanded to imitate God. One of the primary ways that we do this is by imitating His deeds of lovingkindness. It is only by giving that we can truly exercise the divine image inside of us.

Women were created with the potential of imitating God in the two greatest ways possible—by creating new life and by giving of themselves in the development and nurturing of others. As is well known, Judaism values women's ability to bear, nurture, and raise children. It also stresses how important it is for them to be stabilizing forces in their husbands' and children's development. Yet, despite Judaism's preference that women marry and have children, men are the ones who are commanded to marry and to procreate, not women. The preferred role for women is to marry and have children, but Jewish law does not require this of them. Should a woman not be able to, or not wish to develop her potentials as a mother, she still has many other ways of imitating God and actualizing herself as a Jewess.

Whereas the most desirable goal in secular society may be for women to imitate men, the highest goal for both Jewish men and women is to imitate God. As long as a woman's goal is ultimately to develop herself in order to serve God, not herself, many paths are open to her. This is not the case for a man, for whom Judaism proposes that he can never fully actualize himself without being married and having children.

From *To Be a Jewish Woman* (Jason Aronson, 1992).

From a Jewish perspective, should a woman choose to take on the challenge of having children, her job is not simply to be a "baby machine." Rather, it is to create and mold a Jewish body and soul who will carry on the mandate of perfecting the world in accordance with God's will.

LISA AIKEN is a psychotherapist in private practice in New York. She became a *ba'alat tshuvah,* or newly observant Jew, at age eight. A frequent lecturer on relationships and Jewish tradition, she is the author of *To Be a Jewish Woman* and *Beyond Bashert: A Guide to Dating and Marriage Enrichment.*

To Forge His Own Jewish Commitment

RACHEL ADLER

RACHEL ADLER was married to an Orthodox rabbi in 1976 when she wrote a short article for *Lilith* magazine describing her life as a Jewish woman. Most of the essay detailed the struggle between her commitment to traditional Judaism and her intensifying identification with contemporary feminists.

... My halachic commitment pulls me one way, my feminism pulls me another, and I don't know how to reconcile them. Sometimes I suspect they're irreconcilable. Frequently I ask myself how long I'll be able to live with such a tension. It's grim, but I can't see any alternative. I cannot affirm laws which are morally offensive to me without being a liar, while to be a feminist at the expense of *halachah* is idolatry. . . .

I find myself in the same bind dealing with my three-year-old son. I am frustrated to think that I'll be sending him to an Orthodox day school where he can imbibe all the sexism I've fought against, yet I am haunted by the fear that I may be teaching him to be an irreligious Jew. I try to give him both sets of values. I tell him stories about the mothers and fathers of the Jewish people, teach him that God both incorporates and transcends masculinity and femininity, and show him by example that women as well as men learn, daven, and do the mitzvot that define a Jew. . . .

Most of all, I ask myself how I can justify giving my child values which I myself can't reconcile. Do I want him to inherit my tug-of-war?

I console myself that he may very well take after his father, who is troubled by these questions as befits a man of principle, but has managed to pre-

From "Ten Women Tell . . . The Ways We Are," *Lilith,* Winter 1976/77.

51

serve the wholeness of his Orthodox faith. It is probably wrong and futile anyway to try to feed a child a predigested faith. I keep hoping that if I tell him the truth as I see it and, more importantly, show him how his father and I are always struggling with the Torah, I'll be giving him the tools with which to forge his own Jewish commitment.

Twenty-two years later, Adler is one of America's leading feminist theologians, author of *Engendering Judaism: An Inclusive Theology and Ethics*. She teaches at the University of Southern California and Hebrew Union College–Jewish Institute of Religion in Los Angeles. When she was approached about including part of her *Lilith* essay in this book, she showed the essay to her now-grown-up son, Amitai Adler. As his response demonstrates, he did indeed take in his parents' struggle over Judaism—and found it nourishing.

I have never seen such accurate worrying in my life. I was just remarking . . . the other day in a conversation about religion that if I had not gotten at home what I got from you and Abba—in terms of Judaism—if my only experience of it had come from [Orthodox day school], there is a real decent chance I might be an atheist today. . . . [I]t was almost exclusively the fact that you and Abba both (and I emphasize both, since I cannot recall a time when I didn't know there were serious things in Judaism you and Abba disagreed on) seemed to so love Judaism and wrestle with it so much that gave me attachment and hope to carry me through my agnostic period back home to the fold. You said in that piece that you worry that I will inherit your tug-of-war. Of course, you changed the rules of that game a long time ago, and while the resulting struggle is certainly something you have passed on to me, it is not the religious albatross that you seemed to once imagine it, but an inheritance that I value greatly.

Spirituality Is Practical

Rebekah Kohut

I am in favor of a thoroughly religious upbringing for children. I have had ample opportunity for observing those who have provided various substitutes for religion, both for themselves and their children. I cannot say that they have been very effective, or that the result has produced happy people (in the best sense of the word) or successful people (still in the best sense of the word).

The excuses for neglecting religious observance, churchgoing, etc., have been many—among them, that the religions do not meet modern conditions, that churchgoing is inconvenient, the ritual archaic, and other excuses. These are the objections of so-called practical people. Well, practicality and realism, too, are fetishes like other fetishes, and lead their worshipers as far astray as do the cults of pure moonshine. Nobody collapses as quickly under adversity as does the "practical man."

Spirituality, on the other hand, is really and intensely practical. It is the ordered discipline of the spirit that enables people to meet any fate and to rise above the hazards of fortune. . . . Ritual serves as a touchstone. Ceremonies at the synagogue or church, the lighting up of the Sabbath candles at home on Friday evenings—these are not, in themselves, all in all. Rather, they are the keys that open the gates for the flooding of the spirit with the true verities—prayer, humbleness before God, a banishment of the strifes, the vanities, the envies that pit people against one another.

From "A Spiritual Hero," in *More Yesterdays* (Bloch Publishing, 1950).

Rebekah Kohut (1864–1951) was a prominent figure in the National Council of Jewish Women. After the death of her husband, an early leader of the Conservative Jewish movement, she supported herself and her family by writing, lecturing, and teaching. Her embrace of traditional observances while remaining a liberal Jew set her apart from most other Jews of her time.

I Could See a Halo

Rivka Guber

At the time of Israel's infancy as a nation, Rivka Guber, who had joined the British Army during World War II and lost two sons during the War of Independence, was hailed by Prime Minister David ben Gurion as the reborn "Mother of the Maccabees." But there was drama in her life long before World War II. In 1925, when her older son, Ephraim, was born, she could not nurse him, and the baby could not digest formula. So Guber and her husband had to line up a series of wet nurses.

There is one mother whom I shall never forget. That is Rina the Sephardi. She was one of the first six volunteers. When I came to her for the first time, I doubted whether she ought to nurse any child, even her own; for she was thin and pale. We faced a difficult problem. Not a single one of the mothers agreed to give the child the first nursing at six in the morning or the last at ten at night; for those hours are important to the mother, as she needs them for her own rest. Thereupon Rina decided that she would give those two nursings. And so Mordecai would carry Ephraim along to this saintly woman who lived in a forsaken alley at a considerable distance from our own home.

On one occasion there was a really terrible rainstorm. I sat until exceedingly late, waiting for the baby. It was close to midnight before they came. I lay awake, listening to the storm outside, and thought, whence will my help come? The child also kept on weeping bitterly. And then, at five in the

From *Her Children Call Her Blessed: A Portrait of the Jewish Mother,* ed. Franz Kobler (Stephen Daye Press, 1955).

morning, when stars could still be seen through the window, somebody knocked at the door. On the porch stood a woman wearing a raincoat and huge hip boots. Rina had been unable to sleep all that night, thinking how the baby would have to be dragged about again in such weather; and she had decided to come to him.

When she sat on the chair nursing my son, I could see a real halo round her head.

God in the Bursting Seed

Julia Richman

[T]each our little ones true Judaism.

First, God.

Introduce them to the wonders of plant and animal life. *Show them God* in the bursting seed, in the budding flower, in the bird-producing egg, the glorious sunshine. Let them see God and learn to love Him for His blessings in which they share. Let them be made to feel that God means protection, that to Him they owe love and respect and gratitude and loyalty. Make God the starting point and the goal.

A long-time educator in New York City's public schools, Julia Richman (1855–1912) was also active in the improvement of Jewish education and was an early leader of the National Council of Jewish Women.

From "Report of the National Committee on Religious School Work," in *Proceedings of the First Convention of the National Council of Jewish Women* (The Jewish Publication Society of America, 1896).

4

"May the Words of My Mouth . . ."

WOMEN AT
PRAYER

The God of Mothers and Children

Amy Eilberg

I will never forget the first time I was able to *daven* [pray] after my daughter's birth. When I was able to hold the *siddur* in my hands once again, on the second Shabbat of my daughter's life, I found myself reaching out to a different God than ever before.

I found myself talking not to an image of God as the God of law and command and blame . . . I called out to God as the giver of life, the God of mothers and children, of love and care and nourishment, a God who would understand that there was sanctity in nursing and diaper changing and rocking and comforting as surely as there was sanctity in my encounter with the *siddur*.

That night, for the first time in my life, I encountered a feminine image of God, who rejoiced in the birth of my daughter and my own rebirth as a mother. This is a gift that will be with me forever.

In 1985, Amy Eilberg (born 1954) became the first woman to be ordained as a rabbi through the Conservative movement.

From "The Gifts of First Fruits," a sermon delivered 3 September 1988.

Empowered With Grace Bestowed by Women

Savina J. Teubal

In the past few decades, women have revolutionized Judaism with significant innovations, some more meaningful than others. To me the most profound change comes in the act of women blessing women.

In biblical lore, bestowing blessings was the prerogative of the deity, the dying patriarch, and ultimately priests and kings. There is no instance in which a woman blesses another woman. Why is this so?

A deity's blessing bestows supernatural favor upon the individual being blessed. Traditionally it has been the prerogative of Jewish males to transmit in words or deeds the will of the divinity. To bless, then, the giver of blessings must acquire a spark of divine authority in order to transmit divine favor. It is with this authority that a rabbi blesses the congregation or a father his family or child.

Recently it has become commonplace for women to bless each other. When a woman gives a blessing, she too secures the authority to do so and in so doing infuses in herself the divine spirit of transmission. The woman who receives the blessing is not only empowered with the grace bestowed on her but also with a powerful spiritual bond between herself, the giver, and the Giver of the blessing.

Savina J. Teubal (born 1926) is the author of *Sarah the Priestess: The First Matriarch of Genesis* and *Hagar the Egyptian: The Lost Traditions of the Matriarchs.* In 1986, when she turned sixty, she developed *Simchat Hochmah* (Joy of Wisdom), a "crone ritual" for women celebrating the attainment of wisdom that comes with age.

A God Who Is With Us Instead of Over Us

JUDITH PLASKOW

[The] images of God as lover, friend, companion, and co-creator are more appropriate metaphors for the God of the covenant than are the traditional images of lord and king. Defining God's power not as domination but as empowerment, they evoke a God who is with us instead of over us, a partner in dialogue who ever and again summons us to responsible action. Rather than reminding human beings of their frailty and nothingness, these images call us to account as partners in a solemn compact—a compact that demands our response. We do not act most responsibly when we feel subjugated, worthless, and culpable, but when we know our own value, mirrored in the constancy of a God who is both friend and lover, a God who calls us to enter into the task of creation. We respond, not to avoid guilt, but because—as the kabbalistic tradition reminds us—what we do or leave undone as co-creators makes a difference in the world.

JUDITH PLASKOW (born 1947) was a founding member of B'not Esh (Daughters of Fire), a feminist Jewish spirituality collective, and is the author of *Standing Again at Sinai: Judaism from a Feminist Perspective.*

From "Divine Conversations," *Tikkun,* November/December 1989.

May Your Words Illuminate the Way: *Techinot*

Although the writing of synagogue liturgy has long been considered the exclusive province of men and only now are women contributing to contemporary prayerbooks used in institutional worship, Jewish women have been writing prayers for each other for centuries. A tradition of women's personal prayers, or *techinot,* written in Yiddish, goes back to the 1600s. The prayers center on women's concerns, including the three affirmative *mitzvot* for women—the lighting of candles on Sabbath eve, immersion in the ritual bath after one's period, and the separation of a piece of dough when baking challah—the health and safety of children and husbands, and the various milestones in a woman's life cycle, especially childbirth and mourning. Such prayers generally have been addressed to the God of the biblical matriarchs, Sarah, Rebecca, Leah, and Rachel, rather than to the God of the Fathers.

One of the best known writers of *techinot* was SARAH BAT TOVIM, born in the late 17th century, the wife, daughter, and great-granddaughter of rabbis in Russia. (Her pen name, bat Tovim, means "Daughter of Good Men" and is meant to imply a distinguished lineage.) Born into a wealthy family and well educated, Sarah attended synagogue regularly and probably acted as a *firzogerin,* someone who explained the service to women in their section of the synagogue, translating the prayers from Hebrew into Yiddish. She published a number of her *techinot* in a book called *The Three Gates,* which was reprinted many times and survives to this day. This *techinah* is typical of those she included in the "first gate," based on the *mitzvot* women were commanded to perform.

Lord of the world, may my *mitzvo* of candlelighting be as acceptable as the high priest's *mitzvo* when he kindled lights in the Holy Temple . . . May Your words illuminate the way for my feet so that they will proceed along life's

---

From "Hadlokas Ner" in *The Three Gates,* published in *A Book of Jewish Women's Prayers,* ed. Norman Tarnor (Jason Aronson Inc., 1995).

way [successfully]; may the *mitzvo* of candlelighting be acceptable [to You] so that my children's eyes will be illuminated by the Torah. . . .

May our merit of the candles that we have lit protect our children's candles [of life], that they may be illumined in the [study of] Torah.

Many writers of *techinot* followed Sarah bat Tovim, some borrowing her name. One composer of *techinot* during the first part of the nineteenth century was SEREL BAT JACOB, the daughter of Rabbi Jacob HaLevi Segal of Dubnow and the wife of Rabbi Mordecai Katz Rapoport, president of the rabbinic court in Olesnica. This *techinah* was to be recited at the sounding of the shofar during Rosh Hashanah.

May the four Matriarchs' merit, the three Patriarchs' merit, and the merit of Moses and Aaron be present for us at judgment. . . . We beg our mother Sarah pray for us at the hour of judgment, that we may go free. . . . Have mercy, our mother, on us your children and pray for our children, that they are not separated from us. You know the bitterness of a child taken from its mother, as you grieved when Isaac was taken from you. Pray now, at the blowing of the shofar of the ram, so God may remember Isaac's merit who let himself be bound as a sacrifice. Ask for mercy on our behalf.

I beg mother Rebecca to pray for her children and that our father and mother be not separated from us. You know how strongly you long for a father and mother, as you wept greatly when you were taken from your father and mother to your husband Isaac.

Therefore pray for our father and mother, that they may have a good year of life, and I and my children, and good livelihood. We entreat mother Rachel to inscribe and seal us for a good year, without grief . . . We know you

From "Techina of the Matriarchs for Rosh Hodesh Elul," by Sevel Segal Rapoport, in *Written Out of History: Our Jewish Foremothers,* ed. Sondra Henry and Emily Taitz (Biblio Press, 1990).

cannot endure the sorrow of your children ... as when your dear son Jacob was taken to Egypt and afflicted, he fell on your grave and wept: Mother, have mercy on your child. How can you look on my sorrow, when you loved me so much.

So you could not see your child's affliction and you answered: My dear child, I hear your bitter weeping and will always have mercy, and pray for you and listen to your sorrow.

So have mercy on our sorrow.... and pray for us, that a good year may be inscribed for us, Amen.

FANNY NEUDA was a German writer of *techinot* during the nineteenth century, probably from Frankfurt am Main. A volume of her prayers and private meditations, *Stunden der Andacht,* was first published in the mid-1800s, with an English translation, *Hours of Devotion,* appearing in 1866. Although little is known about Neuda, her volume of devotional writings was popular among German Jewish women through the 1940s. The prayer below is typical of the subject matter on which women have based *techinot*.

O my God! More and more it approaches, the great hour, on which I shall give birth to another being, according to Thy wise ordination. O God! Thou knowest my weakness, Thou wilt pardon me, that I look toward that hour with dread and anxiety. For Thou, Omniscient One, alone knowest what that hour shall be unto me. Therefore I call unto Thee, from the depths of my soul: Fortify me with strength and courage in the hour of danger, God of Mercy! grant that the life of my child may not be my death! shorten the woes and pains that await me, let Thy help be nigh unto me in the moment of danger, and do not remember the multitude of my sins. Convert, O God! my

From *Hours of Devotion* trans. M. Mayer (Hebrew Publishing, 1866).

pain into delight at the lovely sight of a living, well-formed and healthy babe, whose heart may ever be dedicated unto Thee. Lord! have mercy upon me! Into Thy hand I confide my life—keep and preserve me from all evil. Amen.

Today, Jewish women are still writing original prayers, often for Rosh Chodesh (new moon) celebrations and to mark the milestones in their lives. GAYLIA R. ROOKS (born 1957), associate rabbi at The Temple in Louisville, Kentucky, wrote this poem in 1991 as part of a weaning service for her son.

Praised are You
Creator of all
mystery wonder and awe
You fill my life
to overflowing,
my heart beats
poems of praise.

Blessed are You
Adonai my God
who has given me
blessings without number
of life and love
and laughter that
sings your holy name.

Thanks be to You
Eternal Source of all,
miracles abound
and gifts beyond counting
my life and breath
whisper an everlasting prayer
of thanksgiving . . .

"Prayer," *CCAR Journal,* Summer 1997.

Vertical and Horizontal

BONNA DEVORA HABERMAN

At the *kotel* (the Western Wall), Jewish women are today denied the right to open their mouths in the song of prayer and chant of Torah because of the prohibition against a man hearing a woman's voice. Surely this is not just a question of law, but a profound silencing of women in the public sphere. As a woman who has prayed all her life, who is committed to prayer, I feel connected to the words, metaphors, images, rhythms, melodies of the *siddur* (prayer book) as I continue to use and to question it. . . .

Prayer has both vertical and horizontal dimensions. We express ourselves to and with our Creator; we speak and sing our praises, our requests and desires, our gratitude. Each of us has a singular meeting, a metaphoric place where we enter alone into the holiness of God's presence. This relationship is vertical. We also affirm—among one another, in each other's presence, and to one another—our faith and our belief. We enact a common experience. We give testimony as a community to God's being and to God's oneness. . . . This is the horizontal plane of prayer: joining together with one another as a community.

The issue of a voice of a woman arises only when a woman is in the presence of a man or men. On her own, and in the company of other women, a woman's voice does not distract; it has the same claim to God's ear, God's compassion. So *kol isha* is a matter of the relationships among men and women at the moment when one is concentrating on directing a prayer to God. It points to where the vertical and the horizontal planes intersect.

From "A Woman's Voice," *Tikkun,* Sept./Oct. 1991.

Let both voices be heard. . . . In the evening transition from day to night, the unsettling moments of entering the unknown darkness of our experience, we affirm together. Not only do we affirm our belief in God, we also affirm our belief in one another. We affirm the holiness of our relationships because God is our God.

BONNA DEVORA HABERMAN, an Orthodox educator, philosopher, and social activist, is one of the founders of Women of the Wall, a group of Israeli women who pray at the Western Wall.

My Entitlement and My Obligation

RIV-ELLEN PRELL

The transforming moment of my life as a Jewish feminist came when I began wearing a *tallit* in 1974. I had found it difficult to make the transition from being able to argue for the importance of equality in Jewish practice to actually living it. I felt somehow unworthy. "When my Hebrew is better; when I know more," I told myself, "then I will be ready." At Chanukah, my friend Isa Aron made up my mind for me, she gave me one.

I don't remember putting the *tallit* on for the first time; it wasn't a moment I ritualized. I simply became a Jew who prayed in a *tallit,* experiencing my entitlement to its sensuous beauty as part of my obligation to wear this garment. My public and unambiguous violation of normative Judaism was linked to my growing private life as a Jew. My *tallit* left me nowhere to hide.

RIV-ELLEN PRELL (born 1947) is an anthropologist and historian who teaches at the University of Minnesota. A longtime observer of American Jewish life, she is the author of *Prayer and Community: The Havurah in American Judaism.*

From "Eureka!" *Lilith,* Fall 1994.

The Difference: Yom Kippur, 5745

Kathryn Hellerstein

Before sunset, when I phoned her, Malka said,
"*A gringer tonnes dir.* Have an easy fast."
"I was young," she said, "my first time,
twelve-and-a-half years old.
There were pogroms, and the Jews
called a fast day to pray for their end.
My grandfather, Reb Dovid, decided
among the twenty grandchildren who would fast and who not.
He chose me, saying, '*Az din vilst, tokhterl,*
az du kenst, zolstu fastn.'
For a whole day I wanted to,
was able to go without food.
We prayed and wept. The air was full of the pogroms—
talk of them, fear of them, the smell of that fear. I tasted
fear. I went hungry. I became a woman."

After sunset, I sat on the right side
of the *mekhitse.* Above the white curtain bobbed
blue yarmulkes embroidered with gilt, an occasional beard.
The posts of the Torah stuck up woodenly,
carried among the men like a darling baby.
A voice from beneath a *tales*

Published in *Bridges,* Fall 1991.

chanted *Kol Nidre,* tentative at first,
in a whisper, then louder, and then a third time,
with the plea of the ages:
Judge us and measure us and atone us for our sins.

Beneath his white shawl the *khazan* led.
The men repeated after him.
Noises of many voices
speaking all at once
between the clean calls:
each man prayed in his own time.
Then the voices joined in chorus
calling one and all.

Among the women, shouts and whimpers.
Needy children punctuated prayers.
The women heard that leading voice
like a warbler through the woods:
we repeated its tune, but it did not sing for us.
We are not the congregation—
that is the difference.
Most of the women sat down
while the men, standing, prayed on.

Mumbling, softly mouthing uncertain syllables,
I give breath, not voice to our prayers.
I am not, in song, like clay in the potter's hands,

like metal in the blacksmith's tongs, like a thread
in the weaver's fingers, shuttling between the strings,
like Jews in the hand of God.

Who will call out the prayers for me
in a companion language?
Alefs, lameds, sofs swam together in the dusk.
I floated on the roll of melody and light,
voiceless as a fish.

This morning I am hungry. I am lost.
I am remembering the dead in their numbers.
Start from the ones I can name, and move out
to the martyrs to God's name,
to victims of a human whim.

The dead wander in, hungry and lost,
coming toward the congregation's voice
as to a lighted window through the snow.
And my voice is small next to the congregation's voice.
A child shouts, hungry, next to me.
I do not know if this is the child of memory.
The child disrupts the prayer. The prayer goes on.

KATHRYN HELLERSTEIN (born 1952) is a poet and a noted translator and scholar of Yiddish poetry. She teaches at the University of Pennsylvania and is represented in many journals and anthologies.

No One Could Have Stopped Me

Bella Abzug

[T]hree times a day, [my grandfather] went to shul, and, when I wasn't in school, he would take me along. I learned the prayers by heart, and my grandfather delighted in standing me on a table and having me demonstrate to his cronies my precocity in Hebrew. Then I would be sent to sit in the balcony with the women. When I asked why, I was told: "That's the way it is." I couldn't accept that.

We were living in the Kingsbridge section of the Bronx when my father's weak heart gave out, and he was dead at 52. I was almost 13, and every morning before school for the following year, I went to our synagogue to say *Kaddish* for him. In retrospect, I could describe that as one of the early blows for the liberation of Jewish women. But in fact, no one could have stopped me from performing the duty traditionally reserved for a son, from honoring the man who had taught me to love peace, who had educated me in Jewish values.

So it was lucky that no one ever tried.

Bella Abzug (1920–1998) was one of Congress's most outspoken liberals and feminists during the 1970s. During the eighties, she was an executive for women's organizations, including Women-USA, a grass-roots advocacy group, and the Women's Foreign Policy Council. In the 1990s, she turned to environmental activism and became a leader in what came to be called "eco-feminism." She is the co-author of *Gender Gap: Abzug's Guide to Political Power for Women.*

From "Bella on Bella" in *The American Jewish Woman: A Documentary History,* ed. Jacob Rader Marcus (Ktav and American Jewish Archives, 1981).

It Was Not in *My* Flesh

Alice Shalvi

Although I have been a fairly militant egalitarian for most of my life, my place and role within an Orthodox synagogue was something I grew to accept. After all, one can praise God as loudly and wholeheartedly from one side of the *mechitzah* as from the other.

It was not until early adulthood that I began to feel a strong sense of exclusion—from the beautiful Sukkot procession with *lulav* and *etrog,* from communal dancing with the Torah scrolls on *Simchat Torah.* . . . I was an outsider, a spectator. It was not in *my* flesh that the covenant had been sealed. But I felt helpless to change the situation.

In 1977, during my first visit to the U.S., I witnessed a bat mitzvah for the first time. This ceremony was virtually unknown in Israel. I was overwhelmed by the skills, the knowledge, the grace, the beautiful voices and the self-possession not only of the bat mitzvah girl herself, but also of her mother, grandmother and sisters, all of whom shared the Torah reading and even the leading of prayers that day. When I returned to Jerusalem and reported enthusiastically on what I had experienced, I was soundly rebuked.

Two years later, I found myself at the annual sisterhood service of a Conservative synagogue in Milwaukee. I was accorded the honor traditionally extended to visitors—an *aliyah.* Only women were present; no infringement of *halakhah* was involved. I accepted.

As I saw the silver pointer indicating the spot in the scroll which I was to kiss before uttering the blessing, tears filled my eyes. For the first time in

From "Eureka!" *Lilith,* Fall 1994.

53 years of my life as an observant Jew, I was seeing the inside of a Torah scroll at close quarters. . . .

For me that first *aliyah* was a distinct turning point, for it made me determined not only to increase my own knowledge and skills, but also to do everything in my power to educate and encourage my Israeli pupils to emulate their American peers and break through the barriers of ignorance and misconception that restrain and marginalize Orthodox women.

Alice Shalvi (born 1930) is founding chair of the Israel Women's Network, the leading advocate for women's rights in Israel. In 1997, she moved from a lifelong identification with Orthodox Judaism to affiliation with the Conservative movement and became rector of the Seminary of Judaic Studies, the Jerusalem branch of the Jewish Theological Seminary.

Judaism As a Spiritual Practice

SHEILA PELTZ WEINBERG

I am deeply interested in what I would call Judaism as a spiritual practice. Practice is an interesting word in English associated mostly with sports and music. Our children have no trouble whatsoever understanding the relationship between accomplishments in those areas and practice. In both sports and music there is a wonderful tension and synergy between the accomplishments and efforts of the individual and the capacity to listen to the other and stay in tune with the group—the team or orchestra. . . . [T]here is an incontrovertible relationship between study and practice, one nurturing and sustaining the other. One is willing to study and practice when one has motivation and sees the results of one's efforts.

Many of our ancestors stopped practicing Judaism. They also stopped learning it or teaching it to their children. The powerful connection between religious practice and learning disintegrated. Many of our grandparents and those who came before them rejected the source of the teachings and the idea that a supernatural authoritarian God commanded the Jews to follow certain laws which separated us from other people; laws that had to be followed exactly one way or else. Others were attracted by the glitter of the modern world and substituted professional or academic training and discipline for religious life. Still others questioned the value altogether of religious practices. Weren't they often performed mechanically? What were they intended to achieve? How effective were they?

From a sermon delivered for Rosh Hashanah 5758.

What would happen if we looked at Judaism as a spiritual practice instead of as a set of rigid commandments? What would happen if we removed the term "command" and translated *mitzvah* as "intention" or "commitment," as a structure that offers the opportunity to awaken to the presence of the divine? What would happen if we said the many practices in Judaism are there as guidelines or directions, and each person is responsible for [his or her] own soul?

Spiritual practices in Judaism run the gamut. We have directions in ways to eat, to work, to speak and be silent. We have extraordinary guidelines in how to rest, how to celebrate, and how to mourn. Our spiritual practices deal with how we relate to nature, money, children, and old people. Our practice teaches us how to embody abstract words like respect, remember, sanctify, and appreciate. All the practices are strands that connect back to the moment of creation, to the idea of a unity and purpose in creation that is of infinite value and needs only to be revealed through our dedication to practice, returning again and again from the expected distractions, forgetfulness, seductions of life. Our practices are consummate opportunities to expand our awareness.

. . . The essence of Jewish spiritual practice is a living out of our highest ethical ideals. The point is not to win a game or even win a case; the point is to be a more compassionate and loving human being, the point is to be more present to the divine light in every moment of creation, the point is to be kinder and more honest to oneself and others. The point is to play in a symphony that we call community and lend one's specialness to the common work of justice—caring for the weak and the powerless, healing the sick and raising the fallen.

There is an extraordinary root in Hebrew, Aleph-Mem-Nun: Amen. Its original meaning, as in other Semitic lanugages, is "strong, persevering, steady." . . . The second meaning of Aleph-Mem-Nun: Amen, in the Bible, is "truth." When the congregation asserts that all that has been said is true, we say "Amen."

I think it is instructive that the same root can move between the concept of strength and steadiness, justice and honesty, faith and practice. I think we have in these three letters—amen—the secret of Jewish spiritual practice. The word for "faith" [*emunah*] is inextricably bound up with practice and behavior. Spiritual practice entails peeling off layers of falsehood, illusion, and deception. It requires a steadfastness and regularity, a community of comrades and colleagues who support us when our own commitment flickers. It is grounded in the wisdom that knows that each small step requires a choice and takes courage. It understands that one primary goal of a spiritual practice is not to make us believers (*maaminim*) in some dogma or doctrine but to make us men and women who are *aminim*—trustworthy and reliable individuals.

Rabbi Sheila Peltz Weinberg (born 1946), a writer of many liturgical pieces for the Reconstructionist movement, is spiritual leader of the Jewish Community of Amherst (Massachusetts). The preceding excerpt was from a sermon she gave on Rosh Hashanah 5758.

"Please Forgive Me"

Joan Rivers

Comedienne JOAN RIVERS (born 1933) was still living at home in Larchmont, New York, at age twenty-six, trying to get her career in show business off the ground, when she and her parents got into a terrible fight and she stormed out of the house. She spent a few days at the Y ("hell for this Jewish princess"), then was taught the art of beating a hotel bill by her boyfriend, an aspiring actor. As it happened, she left home a couple of weeks before the High Holidays.

For the first time in my life I was away from home on [Yom Kippur] . . . Every Manhattan temple was jammed, so I ended up in an obscure synagogue in the Bronx where I told them I was from out of town and they took me in.

It was a humble temple, deeply Orthodox, the service entirely in Hebrew, the men in black hats and yarmulkes and prayer shawls. For me it was like returning to the seventeenth century. I was segregated upstairs in the balcony with the women and girls in hats and babushkas, all of them touching and smiling with bright eyes and reaching past others to grip a hand or to wave—a vast family reuniting on this profoundly important, deeply thoughtful night. I sat alone with a hankie on my head and tears on my face. Somebody passed me a Hebrew prayer book I could not read. I was a stranger.

The service began—very theatrical, musically magnificent, incredibly moving, the taproot of everything I longed to believe. I had been taught since childhood that your family is your secure foundation . . . and to be away from my family on Yom Kippur was the sin of sins.

From *Enter Talking,* by Joan Rivers with Richard Meryman (Delacorte Press, 1986).

The reader intoned:

> O Lord our God, help us to see ourselves as Thou seest us. Make us conscious of our sins and failings; cause us to turn from our evil ways. Give us strength to make amends for our wrongdoing and grant us pardon for our sins.

I was flayed by guilt, accusations out of control in my head: *How could you have done this to your family—sucked them into your unhappiness—tortured them. You are self-centered, a spoiled brat who broke away in the meanest way. What if your parents died this year?*

I knew my mother, who never wept, would be crying somewhere in temple—crying like me because we were split on Yom Kippur . . . Yom Kippur was the one precious night of the year when we existed as a family, when we all came hurrying home, all got dressed up and looked wonderful, and all four of us walked into temple together, appearing to the world happy and united. It was our one night of solidarity. Then at sundown we would return to our home with our guests . . . But on this night I would be sneaking into some hotel room with a boy my mother hated.

To me, personally, in my head, God that night was deciding what I deserved in the coming year, and, as always, I prayed and prayed, *Please forgive me, please put me down for A+ on next year's blank pages.* At the end of the service, everybody turned to one another, smiling and touching, wishing each other happiness in the coming year. When they turned to me, here was somebody they did not know and I felt like an interloper, felt alone and lost. I did not have a person to hold hands with tightly while I made my prayer, *Please, God . . .*

Thankfulness for Being Alive

Nan Fink

As I experimented with meditation and spent more time by myself, I began to feel the desire to pray every day. I remembered how I had felt among the boulders in France, when I had done the morning Shabbat service. That had been one of the most deeply satisfying spiritual experiences of my life. Was there some way I could bring the same combination of prayer and meditation into my daily life?

Once the question was posed, the answer appeared. Without forethought, I picked up my daily prayer book one morning and made my way through the service. Instead of saying all the words, I took the theme of each section, and prayed or meditated on it. It worked. Just as I had found a deep sense of peace in France, I found it in my own house. I didn't need the crashing waves or the warmth of stone.

Thus I began a spiritual practice that continues even now:

The morning light comes through my bedroom window, and I rise from bed, stretching, aware of my body, giving thanks that I am alive.

I notice the beauty outside, the olive tree in the wind, the bamboo, the little hummingbird, and I contemplate the fullness of the universe.

I focus on the passing of time, reflecting on the morning light that comes after darkness, just as darkness comes after light.

My awareness shifts to the divine love that exists in all life, and I express my gratitude.

From *Stranger in the Midst: A Memoir of Spiritual Discovery* (BasicBooks, 1997).

The wave of the Sh'ma begins to pass through me. I say the words aloud: *Sh'ma Israel, Adonoi Eloheinu, Adonoi Ehad.*

As the wave recedes, I name my commitments and responsibilities. This is what I give back to the universe in gratitude for all that I receive. I enter the most intimate moment, the Amidah. I praise God and express whatever is deepest in my heart, my despair, my needs, my hopes, my dreams, and I end with thankfulness.

Finally, I reconnect with community, acknowledging the pain that exists and imagining a world that is healed. As I commit myself to do this work along with others, I say, "Amen."

DR. NAN FINK (born 1940) is the author of *Stranger in the Midst: A Memoir of Spiritual Discovery* and co-director of Chochmat haLev, a center of Jewish meditation in the San Francisco Bay area.

5

Healing the World
GOOD WORKS IN A JEWISH CONTEXT

God Rejects Those Who Supinely Sit

GRACE AGUILAR

Our Father rejects those who do good, trusting in their own righteousness to save them, looking to their own works to purchase redemption; but He equally rejects those who supinely sit, contented to trust in His word, and think nothing depends upon themselves. As works without faith are unacceptable, so equally is faith without works.

Englishwoman GRACE AGUILAR (1816–1847) wrote a theological book, *The Spirit of Judaism,* that captured a wide audience of Jews and Christians on both sides of the Atlantic.

From *The Spirit of Judaism* (The Jewish Publication Society, 1842).

The Power of Direct Connection

SUE LEVI ELWELL

We reach out to others through our own pain, both in spite of it and because of it. . . . For many of us, it is easy to write a check, to send a donation, to reach into our pockets to support Jews at home and abroad, to aid any who lack the essentials of life, regardless of who they are or where they live, but have we lost the power of direct connection? Do we have difficulty translating our commitment to *tikkun olam* into everyday acts? . . .

This day [Rosh Hashanah] is a day of listening, perhaps with a new severity, a renewed attention. Can we listen to one another with the same attention that we accord to the *shofar*? Will we let the raucous *shofar* blasts startle us out of our complacency? Might we be able, maybe for the first time, to listen to our own voices and hear our own truths? For when we can hear our own breathing, our own heartbeats, the sound of our own blood pulsing through our veins, then we can begin to hear the essential humanity of those around us. Their cries, and moans, and laughter, will no longer be muted by the cacophony of our daily lives. . . . Will we hear those around us who have been silent and silenced? Will we hear those who have been forgotten? Will we hear those who call for justice? . . .

On this day of remembering, we shall remember. On this day of judgment, we will seek to become bringers of justice. On this day of listening, we will try very hard to listen to the still, small voice that inspires us toward acts of loving-kindness. And through such acts each of us can save the world.

From "Rosh Hashanah Sermon, 24 September 1987."

Cofounder of the Los Angeles Jewish Feminist Center, SUE LEVI ELWELL (born 1948) is currently assistant director of the Union of American Hebrew Congregations' Pennsylvania Council. The preceding passage was from a 1987 Rosh Hashanah sermon.

Too Many Heads for One Judith

EMMA GOLDMAN

A Socialist Revolutionist, [my friend Chaim Zhitlovsky] was also an ardent Judaist. He never tired of urging upon me that as a Jewish daughter I should devote myself to the cause of the Jews. I would say to him that I had been told the same thing before. . . . I repeated to Zhitlovsky what I had related to the other: that at the age of eight I used to dream of becoming a Judith and visioned myself in the act of cutting off Holofernes' head to avenge the wrongs of my people. But since I had become aware that social injustice is not confined to my own race, I had decided that there were too many heads for one Judith to cut off.

EMMA GOLDMAN (1869–1940) was already a social activist when she emigrated to the United States at age seventeen. She became such a visible leader of the American anarchist movement that in 1920 she was deported to her native Russia.

From *Living My Life* (Knopf, 1931).

The Strength That Authenticity Gives You

BETTY FRIEDAN

[Once] we broke through to authenticity as women, which our generation began to do, we said we would not buy someone else's definition of what being a woman is. I am a person, and what I am as a woman is all of me, not just part of that will give birth, but my brain and my mind, and I need to be able to move into society as the person, myself, and not just as my children's mother, my husband's wife. And then we began to write our own names as people to define ourselves, and to know the strength that authenticity gives you.

We didn't have that sense of authenticity from our Jewish experience if we grew up as I did in an assimilated, almost anti-Jewish community. There was the fixing of noses, the changing of names.

I remember becoming very strongly aware of this at Smith. There were four wealthy Jewish girls from Cincinnati in the house where I lived in 1939. There was a petition to the president of the U.S. to open immigration, to relax the quotas that were keeping persecuted people out. The president of Smith College indicated that he would open the doors of the college to women escaping Nazi persecution.

It was my freshman year at Smith, and at the discussion in the house meeting about whether to support the petition—a few obviously liberal young women spoke up for this, and the Jewish girls, the upper class, were silent. I was new, but I spoke up for it, of course. It didn't pass. But the peti-

From "Jewish Roots: An Interview with Betty Friedan," *Tikkun,* Jan./Feb. 1988.

tion was left on the hall table, so anyone could sign it individually. I signed it, and these two or three WASP girls signed it. Every day I'd come in from the library or wherever, and I'd look at that petition to see if the girls from Cincinnati had signed it, and they hadn't.

I was studying with Kurt Lewin and from his teaching, I began to understand the dynamics of the anti-Semitic Jew. So I was very strong about Jewish identity; in my years of agnosticism and atheism, we always had Passover.

BETTY FRIEDAN (born 1921), widely hailed as the mother of the contemporary women's movement, is the author of *The Feminine Mystique* and *The Second Stage*.

Bikur Cholim

Merle Feld

Before our dialogue today
we are going to visit Najah's brother
he was shot last week
passing through a checkpoint

It was dark and raining hard
he didn't see didn't hear
didn't know to stop
the bullet travelled through
the car door through
the driver's seat into
his back down down
to his spleen
the soldiers pulled him
from the car
stripped him naked
they stood him against a wall
blood coming from his back
from his mouth
in the dark rain
naked

To be published in *A Spiritual Life* (SUNY Press, forthcoming).

A passing officer saw,
yelled to the soldiers
Are you crazy?
so they took him
to the military police
and finally finally
after double checking
that he had absolutely no record
to the hospital

Ten Jewish women—an intifada minyan
troop through his living room
crowded with friends and neighbors
paying a sick call on Mahmoud
an ordinary man, a gentle looking man
suddenly with many strange women
standing vigil around his bed
he tells us his story
in the middle of the telling
his wife rejoins us, passing a basket
of gaily wrapped candies
you can't say no—it would be an insult
the story is coming to an end

Slicha, he says, *slicha—*
it seems that after Mahmoud engaged an Israeli lawyer
the soldiers came to the hospital and said

Slicha—now you should drop the case—
we said slicha

We wish Mahmoud a speedy recovery
we troop out again through the living room
past the gathering of friends and neighbors
What? You are not staying for coffee?
no, we can't, we will coffee with
the women of our dialogue group
today we will talk about
What are Our Sources of Information and
How Do We Know What We Know and
How Do We Decide What is True

I leave Mahmoud's house and walk
into the grey February muddy sky
still in the palm of my hand
a gaily wrapped candy

biḳur cholim: the religious mandate to visit the sick
slicha: sorry

The Pushke Lady

Faye Moskowitz

Winter Sunday mornings in Detroit, my father and I would walk to the Warsaw Bakery on Twelfth Street to buy bagels. . . . No matter how early we came, the Pushke Lady was there before us, sitting in a chair safely out of the draft, shaking her canister under our noses. Jewish National Fund, Pioneer Women, Hadassah, milk for Jewish orphans, trees for Palestine—thanks to the Pushke Lady, no Jew would have to slather cream cheese on his bagel with a guilty conscience.

During the Depression, when we moved to a little town not far from Detroit, spring brought the tramps, pale and spindly, looking like plants do when they have had to reach too far to find the sun. Coming home from school, I would often spot a man at the back door looking for odd jobs, slouch hat or cotton cap held in both hands over his chest, hungry, and my mother would feed him: cold potatoes, bread, coffee; we had little enough ourselves. . . . Afterward, she would tell me, as though making excuses, "It's a *mitzvah* to feed the poor."

Our house was a regular stop for pious men in need of a kosher meal who might find themselves without time enough to reach Detroit or Chicago before sundown of a Friday night. . . . What has become of them, those grizzled men in long black coats, poring over yellowed prayer books by the light of our living room window on Shabbes mornings so long ago? My mother would believe they were in heaven now, saying prayers for all of us.

From *A Leak in the Heart* (David R. Godine, 1985).

As a young married, locked into a small suburban community by babies and a lack of transportation, I met my fellow prisoners by collecting door to door for the Torch Drive, the name given to the United Way campaign in Michigan. In kitchen after kitchen, twin to my own, I drank coffee, shared recipes and surprising intimacies with barely postadolescent women like myself. Almost always, I came away with a few dollars in my envelope to justify my visit and the sense that I had performed a *mitzvah* to justify my life.

The children grew, and I collected: Dollars for Democrats, March of Dimes on Roosevelt's birthday, UNICEF on Halloween. Later, the Pushke Lady syndrome became more complicated. When my oldest daughter was sixteen, I took her with me to the Alabama state capital to meet the Freedom Marchers who had walked from Selma to Montgomery. We both still remember the voice of Martin Luther King floating over our heads in the electric air and the long, sober train ride back with blinds drawn and lights out for fear of snipers. I didn't tell my daughter the trip was a *mitzvah* or even that it was part of her *pushke* training, but she knows it now.

Living in Washington during the sixties, we made our home a way station for peace marchers. The spaghetti pot bubbled, and the sleeping bags came out at the drop of a bullhorn. . . . I have met people, perfect strangers, who accurately describe the inside of our house and tell me they were drop-ins for this march or that. *They* may not realize they stand at the head of a symbolic queue that began for me with an old man who carried a prayer book in his satchel—but I do.

FAYE MOSKOWITZ (born 1930) is author of the memoir *A Leak in the Heart* and editor of *Her Face in the Mirror: Jewish Women on Mothers and Daughters.* She is director of the creative writing program at George Washington University in Washington, D.C.

Love Is What We Do

Cynthia Ozick

[T]he universal Creator is necessarily One, affirming the unity of humankind. . . . The universal Creator, as expressed in Judaism, is transcendent, incorporeal, un-imaged, never incarnate, never immanent, never enfleshed in any form imaginable by human conceptual powers. God's nature is hidden from us, and nowhere is this more mightily addressed than in Job—"Where wast thou when I laid the foundations of the earth? . . . Knowest thou the ordinances of heaven?"—or more clarifying than in Deuteronomy 29:28—"The secret things belong unto the Lord our God: but those things which are revealed belong unto us and our children forever, that we may do all the words of this Torah."

The divine injunction, then, is not to visualize, imagine, conceive of, or fashion natural or anthropomorphic replications of those "secret things," but rather to occupy ourselves with the tasks revealed to us: to do justly and walk humbly, to care for the widow and the orphan, to succor the poor and the oppressed, to love our neighbor as ourselves, and—reaching even further than that—to love the stranger. Compassion is all. . . .

All this is why I find the phrase "the love of God" intellectually perilous and spiritually demeaning. It leads inexorably to definition, which is to limit, to objectify—and to objectify in subjective terms. It is what Heine meant when he said that if the stones of the hillside could have a god, it would be in the shape of a stone. Who will dare to offer a portrait or any description

From "Love Is What We Do," *Portland: The University of Portland Magazine,* Winter 1997.

whatever of the universal Creator? (Even the mystical strains in Judaism, which veer from the mainstream in their approach to Gnosticism—and the Gnostics claim to be God-knowers—speak of God as *Eyn-Sof,* or unimaginable Infinitude.) The love of God, in the sense accessible to human powers, lies not in speculation or meditation or imagining, and least of all in delimiting concretization. It lies in what we do, day by day.

And what we do when we do right is not innate: it must be taught, it must be learned. It is a teaching; it has a text, and the text is open to the difficulties and complexities of moral interpretation and instruction. In Judaism the love of God is enacted through right conduct and the study of right conduct; the act of study, concerning itself with the modes of human civilization, is itself holy. The deep study of right conduct is equal to prayer and liturgy; it is the extension and augmentation of prayer.

Our human obligation is not to contemplate God's holiness, or offer our falsifying love to what we cannot understand: that is not spirituality but idolatry. The great teachers and prophets, in every tradition, have always pointed the way not to the unknowable nature of God but to the conquest and rededication of our own nature.

CYNTHIA OZICK (born 1928) is a novelist, poet, essayist, and critic. Among her books are *The Messiah of Stockholm, The Shawl, Metaphor and Memory,* and, most recently, *The Puttermesser Papers.*

Judaism of the Deed

LETTY COTTIN POGREBIN

Mine is the Judaism of the deed. It's the Judaism of Abraham Isaac Kook, the Ashkenazic Chief Rabbi of pre-State Palestine, who saw holiness as an intensified form of life itself. It's the Judaism of the philosopher Martin Buber, who called for "the life of dialogue" and debate, not monologue and dogma. It's the Judaism of Abraham Joshua Heschel, the pre-eminent American rabbi, who came home from Selma, Alabama, and said, "When I marched with Martin Luther King, I felt as if my legs were praying." It's the Judaism of Rabbi Marshall Meyer who, in the 1970s, put his life on the line to protect victims of state terrorism in Argentina. And it's the Judaism of thousands of ordinary and extraordinary women—activists, rabbis, scholars, writers, ritualists, community organizers—who define female Jews as *full* Jews and who work to expand women's role in Jewish life.

What I'm describing here is . . . a rigorous and demanding [Judaism] that asks us to "act Jewish" in the world. . . . It demands that we repair the world, little by little, day after day, by actively pursuing justice and peace, and battling against cruelty and inequity. Also that we speak out about the human condition with the aim of improving it. Abjure *lashon ha'ra,* the evil tongue—slander, insult, humiliation of others. And advocate for the oppressed; not just Jews, widows, and orphans but all who suffer pain and powerlessness—women, blacks, Palestinians, immigrants, poor people— anyone who is a "stranger" today as we were strangers in the land of Egypt.

From "Confessions of a Contradictory Jew," *National Council of Jewish Women Journal,* Spring 1998.

LETTY COTTIN POGREBIN (born 1939) is a longtime feminist activist and advocate for Middle East peace. A founding editor of *Ms.* magazine, she is the author of eight books, including *Deborah, Golda, and Me: Being Female and Jewish in America,* and *Getting Over Getting Older.*

6

Strength From Within

FAITH DESPITE ADVERSITY

The Law Given to Moses Is True

Isabel Martí y Cortés

Christians believe in a God made by the hands of man, who has eyes and does not see, ears and does not hear, mouth and does not speak, hands and does not touch, feet and does not walk; and they have invented a law adapted for their needs which gives them sustenance, and the inquisitors and their secretaries obtain a good salary which sustains them, but the Christians know very well that the Law given by the Lord of Israel to Moses is the true one, and that at the hour of death they believe in the Law of Moses, and so are saved, and that if they would read the Bible without distortions they would all become Jews. . . .

Isabel Martí y Cortés made these remarks in Majorca, where she was put on trial in 1678 on charges of practicing Judaism.

Quoted in "Scorched Parchments and Tortured Memories" by Moshe Lazar, in *Cultural Encounters: The Impact of the Inquisition in Spain and the New World,* ed. Mary Elizabeth Perry and Anne J. Cruz (University of California Press, 1991).

Let Not the Wicked Scorner Mock

Sara Coppia Sullam

O Lord, You know my inmost hope and thought,
You know when e'er before Thy judgment throne
I shed salt tears, and uttered many a moan.
It was not for vanities I sought.
O turn on me Thy look with mercy fraught,
And see how envious malice makes me groan!

The Pall upon my heart by error thrown,
Remove: illume me with Thy radiant thought.
At truth let not the wicked scorner mock,
O Thou, that breathed in me a spark divine.
The lying tongue's deceit with silence blight.
Protect me from its venom, Thou My Rock,
And show the spiteful slanderer by this sign
That Thou dost shield me with Thy endless might.

Born in the Venetian ghetto, Sara Coppia Sullam (1590–1641) was an
accomplished and educated woman who became a leader of cultural life in
Venice. Although many people tried to convert her to Christianity, she remained
loyal to Judaism and defended her beliefs in much of her writing.

"O God, You know my inmost hope and thought," as published in *Written Out of History: Our Jewish Foremothers,* ed. Sondra Henry and Emily Taitz (Biblio Press, 1996).

Thank God for the Tender Mercies

GLÜCKEL OF HAMELN

I know that this complaining and mourning is a weakness of mine and a grievous fault. Far better it would be if every day I fell upon my knees and thanked the Lord for the tender mercies He has bestowed on my unworthy self. I sit to this day and date at my own table, eat what I relish, stretch myself at night in my own bed, and have even a shilling to waste, so long as the good God pleases. I have my beloved children . . . How many people there are in this world, finer, better, juster and truer than I, such as I know myself for patterns of piety, who have not bread to put into their mouths! How, then, can I thank and praise my Creator enough for all the goodness He has lavished on us without requital!

GLÜCKEL, whose husband "took advice from no one else, and did nothing without our talking over together," began her memoirs as a sort of therapy after his death in 1689.

From *The Memoirs of Glückel of Hameln.*

Stones Steeped in Sorrow and Tears

Rahel Yanait Ben-Zvi

Here were the stones, holy stones, steeped in sorrow and tears, not mere silent rocks but saturated with Jewish suffering. I stood rooted to the spot. Here were women clinging to the Wall and crying. Generation after generation, burdened with the sadness of exile, their faces turned to the Wall, they had clung to those stones.

Upon my right stood men at prayer: some recited Psalms, others sitting on the floor were bent in silence over holy books. The tears choked in my throat. My arm stretched out and touched the Wall; my eyes closed and my head rested on the cool rock. There were no words of prayer in my heart. Sorrow mounted up in me, sorrow that our destiny was so cruel, our people still scattered in exile, our land still lying waste. I did not notice that now hot tears were streaming from my eyes as from the eyes of the mothers nearby. I stood and stroked the stony surface. My glance passed from the women to the men, and my sorrow turned into bitterness and anger, into rebellion against all this crying. We must no longer live lives of mourning, we must rebuild our land.

I tried to hide my feelings and lifted my eyes to the stones. How marvelous to see the creeping plants sprouting out of tiny cracks in the wall, almost hanging on air. On what could these plants possibly feed? It must be on the tears of the mothers, on the heart's grief of the fathers ever since the destruction of the Temple.

From *Coming Home* (Massadah, 1963).

RAHEL YANAIT BEN-ZVI (1886–1979), a founder of the Labor Zionist movement during her student days in Kiev, first stood at the Western Wall in Jerusalem after emigrating to Palestine in 1908. A pioneer of Israel's Women's Labor Movement and a noted educator, writer, and liaison to Zionist women's organizations in the United States, she was married to Itzhak Ben-Zvi, who became the second president of the state of Israel.

We Carry Everything Within Us

Etty Hillesum

3 July 1942

[W]e carry everything within us, God and Heaven and Hell and Earth and Life and Death and all of history. The externals are simply so many props; everything we need is within us. And we have to take everything that comes: the bad with the good, which does not mean we cannot devote our life to curing the bad. But we must know what motives inspire our struggle and we must begin with ourselves, every day anew.

11 July 1942

Yesterday was a hard, a very hard day, when I suffered agonies. Yet once more I was able to brave it all, everything that came storming at me, and now I can bear a little more than I was able to bear yesterday. . . . I don't fool myself about the real state of affairs and I've even dropped the pretense that I'm out to help others. I shall merely try to help God as best I can and if I succeed in doing that, then I shall be of use to others as well. But I mustn't have heroic illusions about that either.

From *An Interrupted Life*.

I Prayed for Wisdom, Courage, Patience

SALLY J. PRIESAND

Prayer was an important source of strength for me while battling breast cancer. When undergoing treatment, I must confess that I did not always know what to pray for. Because I believe in a living but limited God who does not cause the difficulties of life, it did not seem appropriate to ask now for special dispensation, to beg or bargain with God that my life might be spared. If God is not the cause, I reasoned, then God cannot be the cure.

And so I prayed instead for wisdom not to lose perspective, to remember, in the midst of helplessness, the blessings that I continued to possess, to remain as even-tempered as possible despite being afraid or in pain. I prayed for courage to cope with whatever lay ahead and for strength to sustain the hopes of my family and friends. And in those moments when I felt absolutely powerless, something particularly difficult for a person as independent as I am, I prayed for patience and the ability to endure a little more. And when I was too weak to pray, I hoped that God's love would envelop me, that God's embrace would bring me comfort and lift me up from the depths of despair.

And for some reason, I kept remembering an episode of the television series *All in the Family.* Archie, who was more a believer than he would ever care to admit, was in real trouble one day, and he just looked up to heaven and said, "Lord, A. Bunker here." That memory continues to bring a smile to my face, knowing as I do that God is our faithful Friend, the One who listens, the One who understands.

RABBI SALLY J. PRIESAND (born 1946), longtime spiritual leader of Monmouth Reform Temple in Tinton Falls, New Jersey, became, in 1972, the first woman to be ordained as a rabbi.

7

To Be a Jew
IDENTITY, CULTURE, BELONGING

The Unity of Spirit and Political Values

BETTY FRIEDAN

[W]ithin the women's movement I began to make the links with my Jewish experience and my own identity, and I began to get more interested even in theology. For those of us who grew up in an intellectual, secular environment, our intellectual map simply did not include theology. It was a desert when it came to spiritual values. Our spiritual values were political values.

However, my feminism has led me to an unabashed sense of the unity of spirit and political values. . . . I have a sense of wanting to know more about the mystery of being Jewish and about a theology that is not pie-in-the-sky and heaven after you're dead.

In my generation of feminists a lot of feminist leadership came from people who happened to be Jewish, though we weren't religious Jews. But the next generation took this taste for authenticity and embraced their Jewish identity. They then immersed themselves—some became rabbis because our new authenticity made us embrace our Judaism rather than deny it or evade it or weaken it.

From "Jewish Roots: An Interview with Betty Friedan," *Tikkun,* Jan./Feb. 1988.

I Was Fed on Dreams

MARY ANTIN

When I came to lie on my mother's breast, she sang me lullabies on lofty themes. I heard the names of Rebecca, Rachel, and Leah as early as the names of father, mother, and nurse. My baby soul was enthralled by sad and noble cadences, as my mother sang of my ancient home in Palestine, or mourned over the desolation of Zion. . . .

I was fed on dreams, instructed by means of prophecies, trained to hear and see mystical things that callous senses could not perceive. . . . Though I went in the disguise of an outcast, I felt a halo resting on my brow. Sat upon by brutal enemies, unjustly hated, annihilated a hundred times, I yet arose and held my head high, sure that I should find my kingdom in the end, although I had lost my way in exile; for He who had brought my ancestors safe through a thousand perils was guiding my feet as well. God needed me and I needed Him, for we two together had a work to do, according to an ancient covenant between Him and my forefathers.

This is the dream to which I was heir, in common with every sad-eyed child of the Pale. This is the living seed which I found among my heirlooms, when I learned how to strip from them the prickly husk in which they were passed down to me.

The writing of MARY ANTIN (1881–1949) was first published in an American newspaper when she was thirteen, months after she arrived in the United States. She published a memoir, *From Polotzk to Boston,* at eighteen, and is best remembered for *The Promised Land* (1912).

From *The Promised Land* (Houghton Mifflin, 1912).

The Wellspring of My Inspiration

Letty Cottin Pogrebin

My Judaism affects everything I do. It informs my writing, fuels my activism, infuses my home life, undergirds my relations with family and friends, my cultural tastes, political agenda, and moral and ethical standards. Before I am anything else in this world—wife, mother, author, feminist—I am a Jew with Jewish values.

Yet I am not considered a religious person.

Raised in a kosher home, I don't keep the laws of kashrut. Jewishly educated for 12 years, I chose not to send my children to Hebrew school. Passionate about Jewish tradition, I disdain traditional Judaism for its treatment of women. An enthusiastic member of a vibrant Conservative congregation . . . I don't attend services regularly. On Friday night, I light candles, say kiddush, and make the *motzi,* but I also drive, cook, write, and shop on Saturday. I luxuriate in the Hebrew language and the liturgy of prayer but when push comes to shove, I talk to God in my own words, in English.

How do I explain these contradictions? With difficulty. How do I reconcile them? I don't.

And I know I'm not alone. For most American Jews, inconsistency is the name of the game. We split hairs. We make our own rules. We define ourselves in or out of Jewish life depending on the context, the issue, the historical moment. We are continually renegotiating our religious commitment, deconstructing Judaism's meaning in our lives, deciding how we will practice

From "Confessions of a Contradictory Jew," *National Council of Jewish Women Journal,* Spring 1998.

117

our faith, when to accommodate to the dominant culture, and where to draw the line.

Obviously, this approach is anathema to the strictly observant. Orthodox Jews don't pick and choose, they follow *halacha* (Jewish law) to the letter, and one can only admire those who, as a result of their correctness, lead exemplary lives. Even though they have 613 commandments to fulfill, I think they have it easier. They know exactly what's expected of them—period, end of story—while the rest of us drive ourselves crazy wrestling with our doubts, weighing the alternatives, questioning, challenging, probing our souls.

I believe it was Supreme Court Justice Felix Frankfurter who defined intelligence as the capacity to keep two opposing ideas in your mind at the same time. If that's true, we Jews must be geniuses. . . .

My particular contradictions are the result of the best and worst of my history. The best—the golden glow of my mother's Shabbat table, the comforting cadences of my father's davening, the sense memories of sweet wine and sour pickles, my father's tallit with its silky tassels, my mother's voice singing "Oyfn Pripitchek," the thrill of my Bat Mitzvah, the warmth of our family Chanukah celebrations and Pesach seders and heated debates on everything, from the siddur to socialism to Sophie Tucker—all this gifted me with a host of positive feelings about Jews and Judaism. However, the worst also left its mark.

As an adolescent, at a time of great personal sorrow and vulnerability, the sexism of formal Judaism—being excluded from the minyan at my mother's memorial service—cut me to the core and left me disaffected and estranged from faith and community. My return trip—a circuitous journey through text study and Jewish feminism—has been an education in spiritual renewal, intentionality, and consciousness. En route, I've had to refine my beliefs and revisit Jewish sources, gaining, in the process, a deeper appreciation for the richness of our heritage. There is nothing more impressive than Judaism's uncanny contemporary relevance and elastic adaptability, and the clarity and wisdom with which voices from the past speak to the needs of the present. The gradual negation of my negation has made me a more serious Jew—still a feminist agitator, but at peace with my contradictions and at one with my God.

To those who measure religiosity according to whether a person turns off the phone on Shabbat, I am not a "real" Jew. Nonetheless, I work hard at being a good Jew. My religion is not about doctrine, it's about doing. It's about putting Jewish ethics into practice and making sure that "Jewish identity" is not just a label but a badge of decency, not just an accident of birth but a guarantor of compassion and commitment. . . .

Being Jewish is the wellspring of my inspiration. Acting Jewish is something I do out of gratitude, not fear. Living Jewish directs me beyond the letter of the law into its spirit. While I continue to grapple with my contradictions, the greater challenge in my view is to keep struggling to become, in the words of the philosopher Franz Rosenzweig, "a Jewish human being." In stasis lies stagnation. In struggle, there is life.

I Have a Past, Present and Future

Anne Roiphe

I was ankle-deep in middle age, wading down the waters of assimilation, when I discovered that being Jewish was more than I had ever dreamed. How lucky for me. Now I mark the calendar with the Jewish cycle of celebrations, my table turns with Seder plate, Challah bread, and honey for the New Year. I've learned the whole story. I learned where Chelm, the town of fools, lies on the map. I can tell you wild tales about Jewish gangsters in Chicago and Jewish soldiers in the Czar's army. I expanded my family. Freud and Einstein are cousins of mine, so are Rashi and Maimonides. Once I knew only about Jewish catastrophe; now I can tell a Jewish joke (not so well), and I have seen Torah pointers, cups for Elijah and menorahs made of clay.

I am the same old feminist I always was. I am still a left-of-center, First Amendment, anti-war sort of person. I am the same former field hockey player chasing the ball, socks falling down. But now I have pictures in my mind of the destruction of the Temple, of the exile from Spain, of transport trains. I know the stories of Glückel from Hameln and Rabbi Nachman of Bratslav. I have seen tomatoes growing in the Negev and can imagine the Baal Shem Tov dancing in the forest. I am no longer the child who asks what has this to do with me. . . .

Today I frequently argue with a God whose existence I question, but I think that the Jewish people has a purpose, a destiny, a reason for being, perhaps only in the wonder of our plot, the continuing effort to make us shape

From "What Being Jewish Means to Me," *New York Times,* September 12, 1993.

up, behave decently, look at ourselves with a moral eye. I am no longer a mere particle of genetic material spinning out a single life span. I have a past, present and future among my people. Am I ever surprised!

Novelist ANNE ROIPHE (born 1935), author of *Up the Sandbox!* and *Lovingkindness,* has written several books and numerous articles on Jewish identity.

This Ancient Past Had Me by the Throat

Anzia Yezierska

Born in Russian Poland, Anzia Yezierska (c. 1885–1970) came to America as a child, used the opportunities of the New World to resist what she saw as the patriarchal restrictions Judaism put on women's lives, and, after years of struggle and poverty, became a successful writer of fiction that depicted, from the inside, the roiling world of the Lower East Side. In 1920, a film studio bought Yezierska's just-published collection of short stories, *Hungry Hearts,* sending the author from penury to affluence overnight. When her sudden success made her a favorite of newspaper feature writers, she began to receive hundreds of letters begging for money and favors. One from a pious Jew, disillusioned by life in a crass, materialistic America and asking for ship's passage home to Poland, pulled her back to her roots.

The letter had come stamped and dated through the drab routine of the U.S. mail. But to me it was a voice out of time, a voice out of eternity, the blowing of the ram's horn calling Jews to prayer on the Day of Atonement. That homeless old Jew was like a black rock deep under water, pulling me down into its depth. He called me back from years of forgetfulness, from the layers of another life, back to the village in Poland where I was born. . . .

This ancient past that I had despised and rejected with the ruthlessness of youth now had me by the throat. I had never really broken away. I had only denied that which I was in my blood and bones. "Poverty . . . an ornament . . . like a red ribbon on a white horse . . . " Those were my father's words.

From *Red Ribbon on a White Horse* (Persea Books, 1988).

I remembered waking up before dawn in our straw-thatched hut in Poland and seeing Father at his table of sacred books. . . . We had been hungry, in rags, but the poverty we suffered had been because Father chose to have his portion in the next world. In the depths of our want was glory—pride in Father because he was not like other fathers. He had worked for God as some men work for their wives and children. Poverty had carved his religion on his face.

When and how had all that we had been so proud of in Poland become something to be ashamed of in America? How had we come to feel that to be poor was a disgrace?

Sitting now with the old Jew's letter before me, I tried to pin down the thing that had caused the change. And then I thought: In America every one tries to better himself, acquire more than he started with, become more important. In a world where all was change, Father alone remained unchanged. He had gone on living his old life, demanding that his children follow his archaic rituals.

And so I had rebelled. I had defied God. Defied heaven in the next world. I wanted life in this world.

My revolt had grown from blind protest into the self-righteous force that charged me to desert Father and Mother because I wanted to cut loose from their strangling hold. . . . And now this old man's plea for a place to die had pulled me back to the dim past, to all those I had abandoned to become a writer. Like a runner who runs a race in a curved track and must get back to his starting point, the distance I had covered running away to live my life with pencil and paper had brought me back to where I had started.

My Link to Judaism

Susan Seidelman

I've inherited [a] sense of irony from my father's family. His mother was agnostic. Judaism to her meant being political and intellectual; Jewish traditions were nothing more than superstitions of an older generation. She used to show me pictures of my great-grandmother, who bought her clothes in London and didn't wear a wig like other Jewish women of her time. My grandmother was proud of the fact that her family was modern and not religious.

Yet my father's parents never denied that they were Jews. They wanted to drop Jewish rituals, but they felt a strong attachment to Jewish culture. Since Jews were excluded from every society they lived in, they developed their own culture; it was that culture that infused the personalities of my father's family. They were sharp, ironic, and funny. They had a certain sensibility that came from being outsiders. They were observers, with a distinctly Jewish view of the world. . . .

[T]he so-called "modern" Judaism I saw while growing up didn't appeal to me . . . I called it country-club religion: It seemed that people belonged to a synagogue only because they needed a place to throw their daughter's sweet sixteen party. All the high holidays meant to me was getting a day off from school and wearing a nice dress.

Since I found suburban Jewish experience unstimulating and I couldn't identify with . . . ritualistic Judaism, I had no positive feelings for my Jewish

---

From "Irony," in *The Invisible Thread*.

identity. But as I got older and started questioning where I came from and who I am, I realized that a part of me can relate to the long line of Jews who preceded me. My link to Judaism is the Jewish culture I acquired from my father's side of the family. My personality, my identity as an outsider . . . and my sense of humor are uniquely Jewish. That's my Jewish heritage.

Susan Seidelman (born 1952) is the director of the films *Desperately Seeking Susan* and *Making Mr. Right*.

A Genuine Partner of God

Lydia Kukoff

What I liked most about Judaism was that it was oriented toward *this* life and *this* world in a very real way. It seemed to give its followers a system to live by, a system that at the same time had legal, spiritual, moral, and ethical components that were inseparable from the religion itself. Judaism never asked that things be accepted purely on faith. It gave each person an active role to play in the world as a genuine partner of God. Judaism emphasized living with my fellow people in *this* world, but also contained a deeply spiritual element which nourished and nurtured me. I was also drawn to Judaism because of its formidable and wonderful intellectual tradition, its sense of history and antiquity, its connection with an unbroken chain of people and traditions spanning almost 4,000 years! What a people! What a faith!

Lydia Kukoff (born 1942), an early leader of Reform Jewish Outreach, the Reform movement's ongoing effort to encourage participation in Jewish life and conversion to Judaism by persons not born Jewish, is the author of *Choosing Judaism,* a book about conversion to Judaism.

From *Choosing Judaism* (Union of American Hebrew Congregations, 1981).

A Sense of Belonging

TRUDI ALEXY

TRUDI ALEXY (born 1928) left Czechoslovakia with her parents in 1938. They stayed a jump ahead of the Nazis, embracing Catholicism as part of their camouflage, and lived in Spain for two years until a relative brought Alexy and her family to America in 1941. In her book *The Mezuzah in the Madonna's Foot,* Alexy tells her story, writes of other Jews who survived World War II in Spain, and describes the relationship Spain has had with its Jews since the 1492 expulsion.

The more I learned about the Marranos and their stubborn efforts to maintain their essential connection to their spiritual wholeness, the more I identified with them, or, perhaps more precisely, the more I longed to be one of them. *They* had something deep inside that kept alive their link with one another and with their heritage, even under the most stressful circumstances. I, on the other hand, never saw myself as anything but a failed, flawed outsider during all the years I practiced Catholicism and long after I stopped doing so, cut off, forever banished from my own people because there had never been anything experiential in my own past to bind me to Jews. More than anything I longed to have what the Marranos had: a sense of *belonging*.

Alexy left the Catholic Church as a young adult and drifted without religious affiliation for years. Eventually, she found her way back into Jewish life.

From *The Mezuzah in the Madonna's Foot* (Simon & Schuster, 1993).

When I got to the Western Wall and saw the throng of Orthodox Jews praying before it, the old feeling of alienation, of not belonging, again enveloped me. For a long time I stood apart, reluctant to get close. When the crowd thinned out I slowly walked up to the wall and passed my fingers over the worn stones. I was intensely moved by a sense of history, of continuity that unites all Jews in this unique place. I was also painfully aware that I did not know what to do, what to say, what to pray. . . .

Earlier I had written two wishes on a piece of paper I wanted to tuck into a crack in the wall. I stopped to add a third: "Next time, I want to feel I belong." Among the thousands of paper wishes I found a tiny open space and inserted my own, pushing it in firmly so it would not fall out.

When I returned to Jerusalem eighteen months later, and once more visited the wall, I no longer felt like a stranger. . . . I was born a Jew. I now live as a Jew.

It's a Tricky Question

ORA YARDEN

When I was growing up, Judaism was explained to us mostly as a religion. I was taught that whatever happened in the past happened to a different nation. In Israel we were building everything new—a new people, the Israeli kind. The emphasis was on being Israeli, not Jewish. It was the denial and guilt about the Holocaust and what happened to all our people. Our parents were separated from their home countries very rudely, very suddenly. They wanted to believe that here everything was whole, they didn't want to acknowledge the loss. Right after the Holocaust it was generally accepted that Jews went to be killed "like sheep to the slaughter." Years later, studies showed they didn't go like sheep to the slaughter and that you can't judge them by today's criteria. But the message I got was that I have no connection with the past, I'm an Israeli—period. Or—I'm an Israeli first, and a Jew second.

A lot of what I've done has been in response to this background, checking out what I grew up with, understanding the development of Israel. The way I see it now, I'm a Jewish woman first. I wouldn't be an Israeli if I were not a Jew. . . .

[T]hough Jews choose to live elsewhere, spiritually they are connected to Israel and spiritually I'm connected to them. It's not as if having a connection to other Jewish people means they should all come here, but spiritually they *are* my people.

A native-born Israeli raised on a kibbutz, ORA YARDEN (born 1946) has been a radical political activist since the late 1960s.

From an interview in *Lesbiot: Israeli Lesbians Talk about Sexuality, Feminism, Judaism and Their Lives,* ed. Tracy Moore (Cassell, 1995).

Like the Ten Commandments

Melanie Kaye/Kantrowitz

[M]y class and my older sister's had been given dog tags—issued to NYC schoolchildren, as to soldiers—so that in the event of a bomb, our bodies could be identified. My sister, 7 years old, asked what the dog tag was for, and my mother told her. I listened.... And the next time the 5-bell signal rang for a shelter drill and my kindergarten teacher said, "Now, children, it's only a game, remember, under your desk, head down," I, 5 years old, stood up and said it was not a game, it was about dropping bombs on children and they our own government had dropped bombs on children and their eyes had melted and people were burned and killed. The other 5-year-olds began crying and screaming, and the principal summoned my mother to school. "What are you, crazy, telling a kid things like that," the principal is reputed to have said, and my mother to have answered: "I will not lie to my children."

... This was my Jewish upbringing, as much as the candles we lit for Hanukkah, or the seders where bread and matzoh shared the table. My father had been raised observant, my mother, not. But to us breaking religious observance was progressive, the opposite of superstitious; when we ate on Yom Kippur, it never occurred to me that this was un-Jewish. I knew I was a Jew. I knew Hitler had been evil. I knew Negroes—we said then—had been slaves and that was evil too. I knew prejudice was wrong, stupid. I knew Jews believed in freedom and justice....

From "To Be a Radical Jew in the Late 20th Century," in *The Tribe of Dina: A Jewish Women's Anthology* (Sinister Wisdom, 1986).

This is not to say I never heard alternate views, but my parents—though not formally educated or trained in political analysis—had very definite opinions about right and wrong which they passed on to me like the 10 Commandments, ideas I have yet to find wanting.

That this set of principles was Jewish never occurred to me. Around me was Flatbush, a swirling Jewish ghetto/community of first and second generation immigrants, including Holocaust survivors . . . there were clerks, trade unionists, salespeople, plumbers; small business people, radio and tv repairmen, people like my parents and their friends; there were teachers and even doctors who lived in what we called "private houses" in the outreaches of the neighborhood at the point where not everyone was Jewish.

But where I lived, everyone was, or almost. Jewish was the air I breathed, nothing I articulated, everything I took for granted.

MELANIE KAYE/KANTROWITZ (born 1945) is an activist, teacher, and writer, widely published in the feminist, lesbian, and progressive Jewish press. Coeditor, with Irena Klepfisz, of *The Tribe of Dina: A Jewish Women's Anthology,* she is also the author of *My Jewish Face and Other Stories* and *The Issue Is Power: Essays on Women, Jews, Violence, and Resistance.*

Different and Set Apart

EDNA FERBER

I can't account for the fact that I didn't resent being a Jew. Perhaps it was because I liked the way my own family lived, talked, conducted its household and its business better than I did the lives of my friends. I admired immensely my grandparents, my parents, my uncles and aunt. Perhaps it was a vague something handed down to me from no one knows where. Perhaps it was something not very admirable—the actress in me. I think, truthfully, that I rather liked dramatizing myself, feeling myself different and set apart. I probably liked to think of myself as persecuted by enemies who were (in my opinion) my inferiors.

Pulitzer Prize-winning novelist EDNA FERBER (1887–1968), who wrote such books as *Show Boat, Giant,* and *So Big,* faced down anti-Semitism growing up in a small town in Iowa and continued, though she was not religiously observant and did not portray many Jewish characters in her stories, to confront anti-Semitism as an adult.

From *A Peculiar Treasure* (Doubleday, Doran, 1939).

8

"Will Anyone Answer?"

SKEPTICISM AND TENUOUS FAITH

Unbar My Door

Adah Isaacs Menken

I move my pale lips to pray; but my soul has lost her wonted power.
    Faith is weak.
    Hope has laid her whitened corse upon my bosom.
    The lamp sinks lower and lower. O angels! sweep the drifts away—
unbar my door!

Adah Isaacs Menken (1835–1868), an actress of obscure origin but probably a
Sephardic Jew from New Orleans, wrote numerous religious poems about her
relationship to God and Judaism.

From "Drifts That Bar My Door," in *Infelicia* (1869).

I Searched but Did Not Always Find

HANNAH SENESH

Before I was familiar with the point of view of the prophets, and what, in general, the Jewish religion was about, I instinctively objected to empty religious forms, and searched for its true content and morality as expressed in deeds. Needless to say, I only searched but did not always find.... I was never able to pray in the usual manner, by rote, and even now neither can nor want to. But the dialogue man holds with his Creator, and about which the prophet preaches, is what I, too, have found. I see the sincere, inner link, even if it comes through struggle within myself, and through some doubt.

HANNAH SENESH (1921–1944), a Hungarian and ardent Zionist who moved to Palestine in 1939, joined a British parachute corps and worked with the partisans in Eastern Europe. During a mission to Hungary to warn the Jewish population of their imminent roundup by the Nazis, she was captured, tortured, and executed. Senesh wrote the thoughts above in Palestine, at age nineteen.

From *Hannah Senesh: Her Life and Diary,* trans. Marta Cohn (Sphere Books Limited, 1973).

I Want the Serenity of God-Sure People

FANNIE HURST

It is idle to hypothesize on the kind of me I might have become in another era. Here in my own, certainly, I have not found enough of the answers. Why are we put here in this interlude between life and death, not knowing—except by sense of faith and many concepts struggling through the darkness of the human heart—whence we came and whither we go?

The light of that faith seems to burn for some with a pure and steady gleam. It flickers for me. Why, I ask myself in the flickering darkness ... why? ...

We guess in the misty dark, we think with the faith we muster. We want so passionately to know whence, and thus we create our separate concepts of the Father image.

I pull my faith as you would a blanket up over all these restless queries, covering them. Yet their contours show through my thinking. I want the serenity of God-sure people. Even the doubters must falter as they doubt. ...

Men and women under the duress of sickness and poverty, apprehension and panic, turn prayerfully to catch the eye of God. These are not always the serenity people who live by and in their Father-faith.

I wonder what God's thoughts must be concerning those who turn their faces to Him chiefly in times of calamity. The askers. Give me, God. Help me, God. Do for me, God. Protect me, God. Does God separate them from the givers? Has God too much grandeur to look askance at those who come

---

From *Anatomy of Me* (Doubleday, 1958).

seeking and never bearing gifts? Or is Faith in itself the great meaning, the white cane of groping mankind?

FANNIE HURST (1889–1968) left a comfortable, assimilated German Jewish home in the Midwest in 1910 to live among the factory workers and shopgirls of New York. By 1924, she was one of the three highest-paid writers in the United States, author of a stream of short stories for women's magazines. By 1940, she was the most successful novelist in America, thanks to a string of bestsellers, including *Back Street* (1931) and *Imitation of Life* (1933).

Reason Does Not Suffice

HENRIETTE HERZ

The children, particularly the girls, were not at all really instructed in the faith of their parents, but were constrained to observe its *forms,* i.e. they had to keep all of the countless customs which it—or rather the rabbis—prescribed. Girls had to pray in the Hebrew language, without understanding what they were praying. I remember well occasionally having thus prayed with devotion and fervor, especially when there was a thunderstorm, which always frightened me a great deal. Then I would say lots of prayers–any ones at all—quickly one after the other. Now, of course, Jewish children don't do this any more, since the prayers have been translated into German—but they are no more pious on that account. Their parents, who were still raised in the old way, threw aside the onerous observance of the Jewish customs (in which alone their religion consisted) as soon as they became their own masters. Nothing took its place, and so they lived on without thought of God, except—at most—in times of distress. The children were now raised in the same way. Their parents didn't want to teach them what they themselves did not believe, and so they were and are raised in no faith—no devotion fills their soul, and they cannot pray to God when their heart is oppressed and frightened by immense affliction. Reason, which the more cultured take as their help and support, does not suffice to sustain them in severe suffering. Happy is he for whom, at least later in life, the beautiful light of faith dawns inside, and he is permeated by that elevating, blissful

Quoted in "Rationalism and Romanticism," *The Origins of the Modern Jew,* by Michael A. Meyer (Wayne State University Press, 1967).

feeling of devotion before his death. By the Grace of God this happiness has also been mine.

HENRIETTE HERZ was one of the Jewish women of Berlin whose homes became salons for artists and intellectuals beginning at the end of the eighteenth century. She received a better Jewish education than did most girls of her day, but like many German Jews of the time, she embraced Christianity as an adult. In the selection above, which has been echoed by many Jews in postwar America, she explains her disenchantment with what she sees as the meaningless constraints of traditional Judaism and the sterile rationalism of the Reform Judaism that was beginning to appear.

The Botched Job Your God Has Made

EMMA GOLDMAN

GOLDMAN had just finished addressing a German-speaking audience in Detroit in 1898 when a local Congregationalist pastor, who wanted to hear her lecture in English, invited her to speak from his pulpit. Goldman kept her remarks strictly on the economic aspects of anarchism so as not to attack God in her host's own church, but she was not permitted to stick to her agenda.

The applause had barely died away when an elderly woman rose belligerently. "Mr. Chairman," she demanded, "does Miss Goldman believe in God or does she not?" She was followed by another. "Does the speaker favor killing off all rulers?" Then a small, emaciated man jumped to his feet and in a thin voice cried: "Miss Goldman! You're a believer in free love, aren't you? Now, wouldn't your system result in houses of prostitution at every lamp-post?"

"I shall have to answer these people straight from the shoulder," I remarked to the minister. "So be it," he replied.

"Ladies and gentlemen," I began, "I came here to avoid as much as possible treading on your corns. I had intended to deal only with the basic issue of economics that dictates our lives from the cradle to the grave, regardless of our religion or moral beliefs. I see now that it was a mistake. If one enters a battle, he can't be squeamish about a few corns. Here, then, are my answers: I do not believe in God, because I believe in man. Whatever his mistakes, man has for thousands of years past been working to undo the botched job

From *Living My Life*.

your God has made." The house went frantic. "Blasphemy! Heretic! Sinner!" the women screamed. "Stop her! Throw her out!"

When order was restored, I continued: "As to killing rulers, it depends entirely on the position of the ruler. If it is the Russian Tsar, I most certainly believe in dispatching him to where he belongs. If the ruler is as ineffectual as an American president, it is hardly worth the effort. There are, however, some potentates I would kill by any and all means at my disposal. They are Ignorance, Superstition, and Bigotry—the most sinister and tyrannical rulers on earth. As for the gentleman who asked if free love would not build more houses of prostitution, my answer is: they will all be empty if the men of the future look like him."

No Time for Reason or Consistency

Anne Roiphe

That there are no atheists in foxholes is an old saw, probably older than fox-holes themselves, but I thought my skepticism was like Arnold Schwarzenegger's stomach muscles: practiced, trained and invincible. Then [one] summer my daughter Kate developed a swollen knee.... After several weeks during which the swelling did not subside and she seemed tired and at odds with the world, we went to New York for definitive tests.... During that time I was not angry with God for designing a universe that would so unjustly threaten a small child. I forgot my hatred of YHWH and the years of doubt that had encrusted my soul, and I began to beg, to plead, offering to exchange any-thing for her safety ... The onlooker within scoffed at this crawling perfor-mance but this was no time for reason or consistency. I was simply too frightened. The emergency passed. We were spared. I returned to my usual philosophical positions, somewhat altered by the knowledge that the existen-tialism of my college days was far more appealing when there were no stakes on the table—when one has no hostages to fortune.

From *Generation Without Memory: A Jewish Journey in Christian America* (Summit Books, 1981).

There Was No God, and There Was No Sin

M**ARY** A**NTIN**

One day I found myself the center of an excited group in the middle of the schoolyard, with a dozen girls interrupting each other to express their disapproval of me. For I had coolly told them, in answer to a question, that I did not believe in God.

How had I arrived at such a conviction? How had I come, from praying and fasting and Psalm-singing, to extreme impiety? Alas! my backsliding had cost me no travail of spirit. Always weak in my faith, playing at sanctity as I played at soldiers, just as I was in the mood or not, I had neglected my books of devotion ... and I never took up my prayer book again. America loomed so near that my imagination was fully occupied, and I did not revive the secret experiments with which I used to test the nature and intention of Deity. It was more to me that I was going to America than that I might not be going to heaven. And when we joined my father, and I saw that he did not wear the sacred fringes, and did not put on the phylacteries and pray, I was neither surprised nor shocked. ... When I saw him go out to work on Sabbath exactly as on a week day, I understood why God had not annihilated me with his lightnings that time when I purposely carried something in my pocket on Sabbath: there was no God, and there was no sin. And I ran out to play, pleased to find that I was free, like other little girls in the street, instead of being hemmed about with prohibitions and obligations at every step. And yet if the golden truth of Judaism had not been handed me in the motley rags of formalism, I might not have been so ready to put away my religion.

From *The Promised Land.*

9

Out of the Ashes
CONFRONTING ATROCITY

The God of Children

Marjorie Agosin

They undressed and bound her,
and speaking precisely as diplomats and surgeons
asked her
which God she believed in
that of the Moors or that of the Jews
head hanging and so far away
she kept saying
I believe in the God of children.

Marjorie Agosin (born 1955) is a Chilean poet who has written about female victims of torture in South America and in Europe. She left Chile in 1972 and teaches Spanish literature at Wellesley College. Her books include a collection of poetry, *Zones of Pain,* and a memoir, *A Cross and a Star,* as well as other nonfiction works.

From *Zones of Pain,* trans. Cola Franzen (White Pine Press, 1988).

A Fire in My Heart

HANNAH SENESH

It's the eve of *Rosh Hashanah,* the Jewish New Year. . . . If I could, I would write a few words to my mother. . . . I would tell her how I felt yesterday: I was so desperately depressed that I cried. I felt I was faced with two possibilities: to seek personal happiness and shut my eyes to all the faults in my surroundings, or else to invest my efforts in the difficult and devastating war for the things I deem good and proper. . . .

Dear God, if You've kindled a fire in my heart, allow me to burn that which should be burned in my house—the House of Israel. And as You've given me an all-seeing eye, and an all-hearing ear, give me, as well, the strength to scourge, to caress, to uplift. And grant that these words be not empty phrases, but a credo for my life. Towards what am I aiming? Towards all that which is best in the world, and of which there is a spark within me.

So much for myself. Now what can I say about the world around me— the world that is virtually destroying itself? Or about the tens of thousands of people perishing daily? How shall I grieve for them on the eve of Rosh Hashanah? About the suffering, the pain; the injustice . . . what can I say, and to whom? *He* knows—thus there is nothing for me to say on this solemn evening.

Do I believe in God? I don't know. For me He is more a symbol and expression of the moral forces in which I believe. Despite everything, I believe the world was created for good.

SENESH wrote these thoughts in her diary in Palestine on September 21, 1941.

From *Hannah Senesh: Her Life and Diary.*

The Blood of the Innocent

Isabella Leitner

My heart is beating. Faster and faster. It will be me. The *Oberscharführer* will choose me. I know he will. Along with several others. To carry the dead girl to her grave. I can dig the grave, but please, please don't choose me to carry the body. Have mercy. I cannot carry the dead body. Inside, deep in my being, I am just a child. The dead, cold body I cannot touch. It makes me shiver. Please. Please.

There is no crematorium in which to burn the dead in Birnbaumel. The dead actually have to be buried, out some distance from the camp. It is done at night, in the ominous night, and I am frightened. So terribly frightened. Don't choose me.

But he does. And then the pitiful little band is off to the hill to perform the sacred mission. Chicha is chosen as a grave digger, and four others are chosen to carry the body. We are off to a patch of earth in a foreign land that is soaked with the blood of the innocent, the young, the unfulfilled, the martyred children of martyred Jewish mothers who dared to give life in an age of death.

I am about to slip my trembling palms under the corpse when Chicha softly, compassionately, whispers in my ear: "I will put my hands under the body, and you put your hands on mine." Tears are rolling down my cheeks. Not for the dead girl, but for the goodness that is still alive, that refuses to be buried, however hard the madman tried to still the voice of God in man.

From *Fragments of Isabella: A Memoir of Auchwitz* ed. Irving A. Leitner (Thomas Y. Crowell, 1978).

Rest in peace, young girl. The flickering stars above must be the weeping children of your womb. The womb, the glorious womb, the house that celebrates life, where life is alive, where the bodies of young girls are not carried out into the night. Rest in peace, young girl.

Isabella Leitner and her three sisters, Chicha, Cipi, and Rachel, all young women, were deported to Auschwitz from Hungary in May 1944. Their mother and youngest sister were gassed upon arrival at Auschwitz. Cipi was separated from the others and died at Bergen-Belsen, but the three other sisters stayed together and traveled to the United States together in the spring of 1945, where they were reunited with their father, who had left Europe before the war, and their brother, who also survived the camps.

Silence Broken by Shovels Against the Dirt

Lucille Eichengreen

Lucille Eichengreen (born 1925) was seventeen-year-old Cecilia Landau when her mother died of starvation in the Lodz ghetto. Their father had been killed at Dachau eighteen months earlier. After a week without word of their mother's burial, Cecilia and her younger sister, Karin, walked to the cemetery and, despite being told there was no more space for new graves, went into the administration building to find their mother.

As we entered the huge hall, the strong, sickening odor of decay and death filled our nostrils. Piles of bodies stretched as far as the eye could see, each body placed between two narrow wooden boards that were tied together with coarse string. A name tag was attached to each greenish, decomposing ankle. We searched among the dead bodies of men, women, and children until we managed to find the one that bore Mother's name: "Sala Landau." Her swollen, bare feet protruded from the boards.

Without a word, we moved toward the two shovels that leaned against the far wall; then we went outside to search for a small unused plot. We found a tiny area and began to dig in the dry, stony earth. We spent hours in the July sun, the silence broken only by the scratching of the shovels against the dirt. When the hole in the ground finally seemed large enough, Karin took my hand, and we walked back to the great hall. We pulled and pushed and shoved corpses until we were able to lift Mother's body, heavy and cold with death, out of the pile. We carried her outside to the freshly dug hole

---

From *From Ashes to Life: My Memories of the Holocaust* (Mercury House, 1994).

and lowered her into the open grave, barely big enough to embrace her body. For a few pitiful moments, we stared at the planks and at the exposed feet, not yet able to part with the dead. Then we carefully filled the grave with earth and sand until only a small mound was visible. Using a stick, we scratched her name and dates of birth and death onto an oblong wooden marker that we found nearby. We placed it into the dry soil. We stood motionless and drained, staring at the grave. We had no tears and no prayers for our dead mother.

EICHENGREEN survived Auschwitz, Neuengamme, and Bergen-Belsen concentration camps. Because she spoke, read, and wrote German, at Neuengamme she was sent to work in the office of Sasel work camp, where she memorized the names and ranks of forty-two SS guards. After the war, this knowledge helped occupying Allied forces to charge the guards as war criminals and bring them to justice.

I looked at the German, his eyes shifting hungrily from the cigarette smoke to the half-smoked butts in the ashtray. . . .

For me, the smoke evoked the more painful memory of the black clouds that billowed from the chimneys at Auschwitz and the stench that polluted the air when the crematorium was working overtime. Once again I heard the camp orchestra playing Beethoven and saw myself standing in the Appellplatz watching long lines of human beings struggle silently to their deaths. Before this nightmare could engulf me, I abruptly pulled myself back to the green room.

The German was becoming nervous and fidgety. He could no longer stand completely still. I sensed that Major Brinton was about to play his next card; I had seen him make this move before. His voice was sweet and calm, almost gentle.

"We have wasted hours on you, and since you really do not want to cooperate, we will turn you over to the Russians in Berlin. They have other ways of dealing with you. Or . . . " His voice trailing off, he turned and looked at me. I stared at the German.

The German trembled. He no longer smiled. Several minutes passed and finally, stammering and stuttering, he gave us our answers.

"I was an Obersturmbannführer in the SS stationed at Oranienburg concentration camp—but I'm innocent. I only followed orders." He was perspiring. "It was a work camp, and only those who died were cremated there."

"I understand. You bastards just worked your prisoners till they dropped dead, and then you cremated their bodies. You call that civilized?" The major's face was red with anger. The room seemed to be getting smaller, and I felt a stabbing pain in the back of my head. I wanted to scream. The major muttered, "Damn bloody bastard."

Slowly and deliberately, he removed his revolver from its holster. He carefully released the safety and placed it on the table in front of me. I looked questioningly at the major, then at the weapon. The butt was made of dark wood, the barrel of gleaming black steel. Major Brinton shifted his gaze between me and the revolver in silent suggestion. I picked up the gun with a steady hand and, without hesitation, pointed it at the German.

All during the war I had wished for a gun. I had wanted to kill one German—just one—before I died. Seconds passed; the revolver was heavy and trembled in my hand. The German's eyes avoided mine, but his lips quivered an almost inaudible "please."

I closed my eyes. Almost immediately I heard my father's voice reaching me from Dachau where they had murdered him: "If you let yourself hate too long and too much, it will destroy you in the end."

I put the revolver down, placing it on the table in front of Major Brinton, and walked to the door. Outside in the hallway, I sank slowly to the floor and leaned against the cold wall, remembering . . . remembering. I was confronted with a cruel irony: somehow I still could not justify killing another human being; somehow, I had retained my faith in a just system of courts and juries.

The Jasmine Continues to Blossom

Etty Hillesum

1 July 1942, 3:45 P.M.

Sun on the balcony and a light breeze through the jasmine. As I said, a new day has dawned—how many of them have there been since seven o'clock this morning? I shall linger another ten minutes with the jasmine . . . How exotic [it] looks, so delicate and dazzling against the mud-brown walls.

I can't take in how beautiful this jasmine is. But there is no need to. It is enough simply to believe in miracles in the twentieth century. And I do, even though the lice will be eating me up in Poland before long.

12 July 1942

The jasmine behind my house has been completely ruined by the rains and storms of the last few days, its white blossoms are floating about in muddy black pools on the low garage roof. But somewhere inside me the jasmine continues to blossom undisturbed, just as profusely and delicately as ever it did. And it spreads its scent round the House in which You dwell, oh God. You can see, I look after you, I bring You not only my tears and my forebodings on this stormy, grey Sunday morning, I even bring you scented jasmine. And I shall bring You all the flowers I shall meet on my way, and truly there are many of those. I shall try to make You at home always. Even if I should be locked up in a narrow cell and a cloud should drift past my small barred window, then I shall bring you that cloud, oh God, while there is still the strength in me to do so. I cannot promise You anything for tomorrow, but my intentions are good, You can see.

From *An Interrupted Life.*

How Is It Going to Be in the Future?

RUTH WESTHEIMER

The parents of eleven-year-old KAROLA RUTH SIEGEL sent her out of Germany to Switzerland as soon as war broke out in 1939, and the diminutive woman who would become known to millions of people during the 1980s as Dr. Ruth, the radio and television sex therapist, spent her adolescence lonely but safe in a Swiss orphanage.

In 1945 some people came temporarily to the home from the Bergen-Belsen concentration camp. They were the fortunate ones; they survived. I wrote [in my diary], "So many things and situations are happening that one can't even think clearly about them anymore. Up until a moment ago, Frau Mandel from Hungary was telling us of all the suffering she saw: mass murders, gas chambers, and other horrible things. It is really a wonder that these people are still alive. And then one has to ask oneself, 'And you, a tiny little grain of sand among all that horror, you are so occupied with yourself. Stop making such a to-do about yourself.' "

I began to wonder, too, if I really wanted to be a Jew. Being one seemed to mean so much suffering—did I really want to expose myself to that? Once I wrote, "What are you? What does it mean to be a Jew? Am I a German? Am I a Jew? . . . How is it going to be in the future? . . . Look at the others, what they have been through. Will they ever again be able to laugh? To be happy? I think not. And why all this? Because they have a different faith?"

From *All in a Lifetime,* by Ruth Westheimer with Ben Yagoda (Warner Books, 1987).

Are They "Them" or "Us"?

ADRIENNE RICH

Sometime in 1946, while still in high school, I read in the newspaper that a theater in Baltimore was showing films of the Allied liberation of the Nazi concentration camps. Alone, I went downtown after school one afternoon and watched the stark, blurry, but unmistakable newsreels. . . . [I]t came to me that every one of those piles of corpses, mountains of shoes and clothing had contained, simply, individuals, who had believed, as I now believed of myself, that they were intended to live out a life of some kind of meaning, that the world possessed some kind of sense and order; yet *this* had happened to them. And I, who believed my life was intended to be so interesting and meaningful, was connected to those dead by something—not just mortality but a taboo name, a hated identity. Or was I—did I really have to be? Writing this now, I feel belated rage that I was so impoverished by the family and social worlds I lived in, that I had to try to figure out by myself what this did indeed mean for me. That I had never been taught about resistance, only about passing. That I had no language for anti-Semitism itself.

When I went home and told my parents where I had been, they were not pleased. I felt accused of being morbidly curious, not healthy, sniffing around death for the thrill of it. . . . One thing was clear: there was nobody in my world with whom I could discuss those films. Probably at the same time, I was reading accounts of the camps in magazines and newspapers;

From "Split at the Root: An Essay on Jewish Identity," in *Blood, Bread, and Poetry: Selected Prose 1979–1985* (Norton, 1986).

what I remember were the films and having questions that I could not even phrase, such as *Are those men and women "them" or "us"?*

To be able to ask even the child's astonished question *Why do they hate us so?* means knowing how to say "we." The guilt of not knowing, the guilt of perhaps having betrayed my parents or even those victims, those survivors, through mere curiosity—these also froze in me for years the impulse to find out more about the Holocaust.

Daughter of an assimilated Jewish father and a Gentile mother, poet ADRIENNE RICH (born 1929) married a nonobservant Jewish man from a traditional background and reared three Jewish sons before, in the 1970s, leaving her marriage, coming out as a lesbian, and claiming her own Jewish identity.

Wicked Woman

FAYE MOSKOWITZ

My father married a refugee from the Holocaust soon after my mother died. Left with two small children, he needed someone to care for them. Even my mother's sisters approved his choice. It was a good deed to marry such a woman, one who had "lost" two sons in the death camps. ("Lost," as though she had carelessly misplaced the boys somewhere and might one day remember where she had left them.) "She's been through so much," one aunt told me. "She'll be grateful for anything; she'll be good to your brothers. She lost sons, after all."

So one blistering August day, when even the bluebottles were too languid to buzz, I heard the woman shout at my six-year-old brother, and the words were ripped out of her like so many pieces of flesh, "Why do you live, and my sons are in the ground?" I told that story everywhere in my family, spitting out my own loss and jealousy with every terrible syllable. "Wicked woman," I said to all the sympathetic ears. "What can you expect?" they replied. "Those who survived what *they* saw are animals."

The refugee woman is dead and my father, too, but I still ask her forgiveness whenever I think of that summer day. Out of the unspeakable depths of her loss, the words were wrenched. My brother was there and was splattered by them, but he was not the target. How could we all have so misread her anguish? As if children were interchangeable and one could take the place of another. . . .

From *A Leak in the Heart.*

He Still Had Anne Frank

Roseanne

Every Friday night for Shabbas, the entire clan would congregate in Bobbe's apartment for dinner, dancing and the telling of the stories, which were about how ten years previous, one-third of all the people who looked like us were disappeared from the earth.

There was a big window sill where I created the Las Vegas–style entertainment that came almost mystically to me back then at the age of three. All the family loved my act and used to call me "Sarah Bernhardt." The stage was the only place in Utah where I felt safe. I entertained like mad, because I was afraid if I didn't everyone would start to talk about the Holocaust, while I longed for my childhood. . . . When it would happen anyway, I tried to go into the bedroom and put pillows over my ears, or watch TV with the sound up loud, or sing to myself. Still, I always heard and I was afraid. I didn't understand geography, I thought that these horrible things had happened just down the street, on the next block, very close to me. Now I feel it was even closer than that. It was one breath away.

One particular Friday night, I locked myself in the bathroom and proceeded to levitate around the room, there was a very high window, and rising up to it I saw, sailing through the air, a man on a horse who looked like my grandfather, Ben, who had died a few years before. He was waving at me and telling me to hang on, that I would be alright [sic], that he would see to it that God wouldn't take any more little Jewish girls right now,

---

From *My Life as a Woman* (Harper & Row, 1989).

because He still had Anne Frank. This is the story I see in every Marc Chagall painting.

Sometimes, still, I feel like I could weep, just lay my head in my hands, and let go with some great flood that would drown the world. I am always at the edge of collapse, in this world when I think about how fragile everything is, and how we, like spiders and ants and bees spend our lives trying to create safety, a web, a hill, a hive, and yet there is no such thing, and realizing this, I will, for a while, feel great hollow awe.

Comedienne-actress ROSEANNE (born 1952) grew up Jewish in Salt Lake City, Utah, surrounded by Christians and among family members who often displayed a high degree of ambivalence about being Jewish.

Women Bathing at Bergen-Belsen

Enid Shomer

April 24, 1945

Twelve hours after the Allies arrive
there is hot water, soap. Two women bathe
in a makeshift, open-air shower while nearby
fifteen thousand are flung naked into mass graves
by captured SS guards. Clearly legs and arms
are the natural handles of a corpse. The bathers,
taken late in the war, still have flesh
on their bones, still have breasts. Though nudity was
a death sentence here, they have undressed,
oblivious to the soldiers and the cameras.
The corpses push through the limed earth like upended
headstones. The bathers scrub their feet, bending
in beautiful curves, mapping the contours
of the body, that kingdom to which they've returned.

"Women Bathing at Bergen-Belsen," in *Stalking the Florida Panther*.

One Can Always Recapture Happiness

ANNE FRANK

February 23, 1944

The best remedy for those who are afraid, lonely, or unhappy is to go out-side, somewhere where they can be quite alone with the heavens, nature, and God. Because only then does one feel that all is as it should be and that God wishes to see people happy, amidst the simple beauty of nature. . . .

. . . I long for freedom and fresh air, but I believe now that we have ample compensation for our privations. I realized this quite suddenly when I sat in front of the window this morning.

When I looked outside right into the depth of Nature and God, then I was happy, really happy. So long as I have that happiness here, the joy in nature, health and a lot more besides, all the while one has that, one can always recapture happiness.

Riches can all be lost, but that happiness in your own heart can only be veiled, and it will still bring you happiness again, as long as you live. As long as you can look fearlessly up into the heavens, as long as you know that you are pure within and that you will still find happiness.

July 15, 1944

It's really a wonder that I haven't dropped all my ideals, because they seem so absurd and impossible to carry out. Yet I keep them, because in spite of everything I still believe that people are really good at heart. I simply can't build up my hopes on a foundation consisting of confusion, misery, and

---

From *The Diary of a Young Girl,* trans. B. M. Mooyaart (Pocket Books, 1953).

death. I see the world gradually being turned into a wilderness, I hear the ever approaching thunder, which will destroy us too, I can feel the sufferings of millions and yet, if I look up into the heavens, I think that it will all come right, that this cruelty too will end, and that peace and tranquillity will return again.

In the meantime, I must uphold my ideals, for perhaps the time will come when I shall be able to carry them out.

ANNE FRANK (1929–1945), perhaps the most widely read chronicler of the Holocaust through her diary, was captured along with her family in the Amsterdam hiding place in which they had lived for more than two years about three weeks after writing the second entry above. She died of typhus at Bergen-Belsen in March 1945, two months before the camp was liberated.

Teetering on the Brink

OLGA LENGYEL

I recall endless discussions of student days when we used to seek an answer to the question: Fundamentally, is man good or bad? At Birkenau one was tempted to reply that he was unalterably bad. But this was a confirmation of the Nazi philosophy; that humanity is stupid and evil and needs to be driven with the cudgel. Perhaps the greatest crime the "supermen" committed against us was their campaign, often successful, to turn us into monstrous beasts ourselves. . . .

Each camp, each barrack, each [bunk] was a little jungle apart from the others, but all were subject to the man-eating standards. To reach the summit of the pyramid in each of these jungles, one had to become a creature after the image of the Nazis, devoid of all scruples, especially of all feelings of friendship, solidarity, and humanity.

In Egypt, the slaves who built the pyramids and died at their work might at least have seen their structure, the work of their hands, rising always a little higher. The prisoners of Auschwitz-Birkenau who carried piles of stone, only to drag them to their original places the next day, could see but one thing: the revolting sterility of their effort. The weaker individuals sank more and more into an animal existence. . . . One required an extraordinary moral force to teeter on the brink of the Nazi infamy and not plunge into the pit.

Yet I saw many internees cling to their human dignity to the very end. The Nazis succeeded in degrading them physically, but they could not

---

From *Five Chimneys: The Story of Auschwitz* (Howard Fertig, 1983).

debase them morally. Because of these few, I have not entirely lost my faith in mankind. If, even in the jungle of Birkenau, all were not necessarily inhuman to their fellowmen, then there is hope indeed.

It is that hope which keeps me alive.

OLGA LENGYEL, who had medical training, assisted her doctor husband at his hospital in the Transylvanian town of Cluj (now part of Romania) before being deported to Auschwitz-Birkenau in 1944. Her husband, parents, and children all died at Auschwitz. A note: while most writers of Holocaust memoirs required the passage of many years before writing about their experiences, Lengyel first published her story, *Five Chimneys: The Story of Auschwitz,* in 1947.

Not What God Intended

Tova Berger

After I got out of the camps, I had some very dark moments. I was angry at God for making me suffer too much, I was angry at everything. I hated the Germans, I hated everyone. But through the years I started coming back. I didn't want to forget what had happened, but I had to put things in perspective; I couldn't be bitter forever. I began to believe in God once again. . . .

What happened is not what God intended. Even in the camp I tried to be positive. One time we were supposed to go to the gas chamber but there was no room for us. I always imagined that in the next hour something might happen to make things better. Even as a little girl I was taught that we shouldn't give up . . . that tomorrow might bring a change. Judaism is a very positive religion. Jews have suffered throughout history but we've always had some kind of light to hold onto. We are the people of hope.

Tova Berger was one of twenty-three people out of two thousand who survived the 1945 death march from Auschwitz to Bergen-Belsen. She lived in Israel before emigrating to the United States in 1963, where, at midlife, she earned her high school diploma, resuming the education that had been interrupted by the war, followed by a college degree in nursing and an M.A.

From "Hope," in *The Invisible Thread*.

10

"I Believe"
DECLARATIONS
OF FAITH

Faith Makes One Strong

Hannah Senesh

I think religion means a great deal in life, and I find the modern concept—that faith in God is only a crutch for the weak—ridiculous. It's exactly that faith which makes one strong, and because of it one does not depend upon other things for support.

Senesh wrote these lines in her diary a few weeks before her sixteenth birthday.

From *Hannah Senesh: Her Life and Diary*.

A Well of Fresh Water I Found

Rebecca Tiktiner

I had seen. In my heart I meditated. With my voice I called out. Here, I have now come. And today I walked. And a well of fresh water I found. And I discovered the big stone from the well. And from it I drank. And I was still thirsty. And I said in my heart, I will go and I will bring. To all my near ones. And my bones will rejoice. That they will drink for the length of their days. To fulfill what is said: drink blessed water and you will be blessed by the Blessed. And so with those who are sheltered in Your shade. And so it was promised to us by Your prophets. It will not be removed from the mouths of the seed of your seed. And I also, Your handmaid. The daughter of Your righteous ones. To fulfill Your words. And I shall also come after You. And I fulfilled Your commandments. To follow in Your Torah. Because all of my good, all, is from You. And my resting place is [in] You. And I will look to Your ways. For Your words are a candle to my feet. In order that You be just in all Your judgments. For You are close to all who call out to You. And to all who desire to see You. They will merit resting in the pleasure of Your eyes.

Rebecca Tiktiner lived in Eastern Europe, either in Prague or Poland, during the first half of the sixteenth century. She translated an eleventh-century ethical treatise, *Duties of the Heart,* into Yiddish from its original Hebrew, and she wrote a book in Yiddish of moral teachings and poetry, *Meneket Rivka (Rebecca's*

From *Meneket Rivkah,* published in Cracow, 1618, trans. by William Ungar, published in *Written Out of History*.

Nurse), which was published in 1609, long after her death. Her scholarship moved the printer of the second edition of *Meneket Rivka,* published in Cracow in 1618, to praise Tiktiner as someone who demonstrated that a woman could be a *chaver,* or partner in the study of Torah and Talmud. In the introduction to *Meneket Rivka,* above, Tiktiner compares the study of Torah to a well of fresh water to be drunk from by all who are thirsty.

Though He Tarry, I Will Hope for Him

Rachel Luzzatto Morpurgo

My God, my redeeming rock—
Look and see and hear my voice.
I'll weep, I'll cry, I'll beg.
Oh! Have pity and compassion for a troubled nation.

Help erect my tent.
For no one questions, no one helps.
Sons will return to their borders
Crowned with the world's joy.

I beseech Thee, carry the weight of their transgressions.
Hasten and lift up the nation's chosen one.
O cry no more. For God is gracious.

Though He tarry, I will hope for Him.
He'll build the walls of His House
And Rachel will rejoice
In a new song.

Rachel Luzzatto Morpurgo (1790–1871) was born into one of Italy's most prominent Jewish families and reared in its tradition of scholarship. Her poetry, written in Hebrew, deals with her faith as a Jew and her hopes for the coming of the Messiah and the restoration of Israel.

1855 poem from *Ugav Rahel* (Rachel's Harp) ed. Vittorio Castiglioni, 1943, trans. Elisa Blankstein, published in *Written Out of History*.

Believing Is Seeing

Tehilla Lichtenstein

[D]o not tie yourself down, do not *limit* yourself, to the meager testimony of your senses; do *not* follow the popular proverb, do not confine your understanding, do not *narrow* your belief to the small compass over which the physical eye can range. If you believe only what you see, your world will consist only of molecules and atoms, of inert matter, having little soul and meaning; you yourself will be but a moving mechanism, having neither significance nor permanency, nor connection with the central meaning of things. And where would God be in your consciousness, who is not to be seen except with the eyes of the soul, nor felt except by the sentient heart? But turn the proverb around, and see with your inner vision that which you believe; for *believing is seeing*.

And I do not mean by that that faith makes you see, makes you imagine, that which is not and cannot be, and will never be; I do not mean that faith, that believing, will make you capable of deluding yourself, of mistaking illusion for reality, of being satisfied with illusion, with mere imaginings, and allowing them to take the place of reality. No, I mean that believing is the act of seeing, faith expresses itself in seeing; not seeing illusions, but seeing that which is sought, which is desired, which is to be attained.

Believing in God, for example, is seeing God; seeing Him in the form of those attributes that you believe Him to possess, seeing Him as strength,

---

From "Believing Is *Seeing*," in *Applied Judaism: Selected Jewish Science Essays* (Society of Jewish Science, 1989).

seeing Him as love, seeing Him as guidance, as shelter, as protection, as infinite loving kindness.

TEHILLA LICHTENSTEIN (1893–1973) became spiritual leader of the Society of Jewish Science after her husband (the movement's founder, Rabbi Morris Lichtenstein) died in 1938. She continued to preach to large numbers of Jews until shortly before her death. Her sermons espoused the society's basic concept of God not as an anthropomorphic being or as an abstract force but as a source of goodness and creativity within each person with the potential to bring about happiness and healing.

The Mother of Months Uplifts Her Horn of Plenty

Emma Lazarus

Not while the snow-shroud round dead earth is rolled,
    And naked branches point to frozen skies,—
When orchards burn their lamps of fiery gold,
    The grape glows like a jewel, and the corn
A sea of beauty and abundance lies,

                    Then the new year is born.

Look where the mother of the months uplifts
    In the green clearness of the unsunned West,
Her ivory horn of plenty, dropping gifts,
    Cool, harvest-feeding dews, fine-winnowed light;
Tired labor with fruition, joy and rest

                    Profusely to requite.

Blow, Israel, the sacred cornet! Call
    Back to thy courts whatever faint heart throb
With thine ancestral blood, thy need craves all.
    The red, dark year is dead, the year just born
Leads on from anguish wrought by priest and mob.

                    To what undreamed-of morn?

From "The New Year: Rosh-Hashanah, 5643 (1882)," in *Emma Lazarus: Selections From Her Poetry and Prose,* ed. Morris U. Schappes (Emma Lazarus Federation of Jewish Women's Clubs, 1967).

For never yet, since on the holy height,
    The Temple's marble walls of white and green
Carved like the sea-waves, fell, and the world's light
    Went out in darkness,—never was the year
Greater with portent and with promise seen,
                                    Than this eve now and here.

Even as the Prophet promised, so your tent
    Hath been enlarged unto earth's farthest rim.
To snow-capped Sierras from vast steppes ye went,
    Through fire and blood and tempest-tossing wave,
For freedom to proclaim and worship Him,
                                    Mighty to slay and save.

High above flood and fire ye held the scroll,
    Out of the depths ye published still the Word.
No bodily pang had power to swerve your soul:
    Ye, in a cynic age of crumbling faiths,
Lived to bear witness to the living Lord,
                                    Or died a thousand deaths.

In two divided streams the exiles part,
    One rolling homeward to its ancient source,
One rushing sunward with fresh will, new heart.
    By each the truth is spread, the law unfurled,
Each separate soul contains the nation's force,
                                    And both embrace the world.

Kindle the silver candle's seven rays,
    Offer the first fruits of the clustered bowers,
The garnered store of bees. With prayer and praise
    Rejoice that once more tried, once more we prove
How strength of supreme suffering still is ours
                      For Truth and Law and Love.

Best known for "The New Colossus," the poem inscribed on the pedestal of the Statue of Liberty, EMMA LAZARUS (1849–1887) was born into a wealthy, assimilated Sephardic family that counted several generations in America, but her Jewish identity was galvanized in the early 1880s with the first huge wave of Jewish immigrants from Eastern Europe. Her connection to the Eternal was more tenuous than her bond with the Jewish people, as exemplified in the poem above, "The New Year: Rosh-Hashanah, 5643 (1882)."

My Faith Was in My Body

Faith in the constancy of change and the miraculous ability of our bodies never to be the same taught me to be real, and I learned of Faith by touching earth, I learned of faith by listening to breath move through me, I learned of faith by feeling my ribs and chest soften when the spasms of releasing past traumas brought with them the images of abandonment and sexual abuse and betrayal from my own early life and early family. The faith I found was in my own body as spiritual truth . . .

FANCHON SHUR (born 1935) is a Cincinnati-based choreographer and movement therapist who has created sacred dance ceremonies for communities based on Jewish and world cultures. She is the artistic director of Growth in Motion.

From "My Dance Work As a Reflection of a Jewish Woman's Spirituality," in *Four Centuries of Jewish Women's Spirituality: A Sourcebook,* ed. Ellen M. Umansky and Dianne Ashton (Beacon Press, 1992).

To Become the Best That We Can Be

Cynthia Ozick

The Sabbath is not only not in nature, it is against nature. In nature, all the days are alike—the birds continue to fly, the fish to swim, the grass to grow, the beasts to forage. But the Sabbath enters human history as a creation, an invention, a transcendent *idea*: an idea imposed on, laid over, all of nature's evidences. The Greeks and the Romans derided the Jews for observing the Sabbath—conduct so abnormal as to be absurd, and economically wasteful besides. . . . For the Greeks and the Romans, all days were weekdays. Both masters and slaves were slaves to a clock that never stopped.

The Sabbath stands for liberation—and not only human liberation. Even the ox is liberated from toil on the Sabbath. Every creature, human or animal, is respected for its individual essence and given a day of peace. The Sabbath stands for the brotherly peace of Paradise; it sanctifies by seizing perfection out of the ragged flow of ordinary time. It conveys an understanding of distinctions: that the sacred departs from the everyday and therefore can never bore us; and that, as the Sabbath is unique in the week's row of days, all beings are unique and not to be regarded as drones or robots or slaves of any system.

Holiness means separateness: *kadosh,* the Hebrew word for "holy," is rendered as "set apart." The Sabbath is set apart from routine so that the delights of being alive can be savored without the distractions of noisy demands, jobs, money and all the strivings of ego. Both power and power-

---

From "Remember the Sabbath Day to Keep It Holy," *Self,* December 1997.

lessness become irrelevant; on the Sabbath equality and dignity rule. Only a life in danger can override the Sabbath's focus on spiritual and moral elevation through tranquility, fellowship, study, song, beauty, cleanliness, family intimacy. Every festive Sabbath meal is a holiday of thanksgiving. The Sabbath inspires us all to become the best that we can be. Every Sabbath day is a sacred fulfillment. Every Sabbath is a completion of Genesis: a divine creation in itself, fashioned, through human dedication, in the image of God.

The Darkness Vanished

Paula Reimers

You can bring nothing to the mikveh, only your self.

> You come utterly naked, a physical manifestation of a spiritual reality.
> Naked of all your accomplishments.
> Naked of all your relationships to others.
> Naked of all your defense mechanisms.
> You cannot even bring your name. . . .

If you are truly honest, you will admit that when stripped of all these things, there is not really very much of "you" left. You cannot see why that self should be acceptable to God or the Jewish people.

So naked and exposed, you are in the most profound sense accepting. You cannot be anything else.

And you are, in the same moment, accepted.

You arise from the water, clothed with the mitzvot as a garment of light. Having gone through it, you will never, ever be the same.

I stepped into the mikveh waters—and all the fear, the darkness vanished, as the sun melts the clouds.

Within the water, I opened my eyes:

The water was translucent as light.

I know what the midrash means—in that light, I can see from one end of the world to the other.

"Mikveh Journal," in *Lechem Tafayl,* the student journal of Jewish Theological Seminary, Winter 1990.

I rise above the water. I am naked, but unashamed. I want to ask them all to join me; I know they will not.

I immerse again in the light. I rise. I do not remember the blessings. Lord, if it is your will that I be Jewish, help me, tell me the blessings. I hear the blessings in my heart, and repeat them. Thank you.

And I hear them say "amen," my patient Bayt Din. In all my imaginings, I had never thought about how lovely that "amen" would sound!

Again into the water-light, and I emerge. I see the world for the very first time.

Thank you, Lord of the Universe, Lord of my life, for bringing me to this place and time. Keep me always in your heart, and lead me always in your ways.

PAULA REIMERS (born 1947) converted to Judaism in 1981. A graduate of Jewish Theological Seminary, she serves Temple Beth El in Burbank, California, as its rabbi.

I Will Open Myself in the Water

Noa Rachael Kushner

It is between me and the water now
The water is my medium
With it I inscribe my name
invisible and permanent
The house of Israel becomes my home

Another step of being
a path traced with new eyes

I will open myself in the water
immerse myself whole
And I will emerge
complicated and honest as ever
A Jew

Blessed is the Holy One to whom I entrust the
    transformations of my soul.
Blessed is the Holy One Who has chosen me for the
    people Israel.
Blessed am I, who chooses the people Israel, through
    the water.

Noa Rachael Kushner (born 1970) was ordained by Hebrew Union
College–Jewish Institute of Religion in May 1998.

From "Meditation Before Mikvah," in *Choosing a Jewish Life* by Anita Diamant (Schocken Books, 1996).

God Answers, and Laughs

Judy Petsonk

One starry March night, I stood on a bank of frozen earth and threw out a challenge to Heaven: "If you are there, I am going to act as if I believe in You, and see what happens. If You are not there, then You can't laugh at me."

Early the next morning, as I jogged along the unfinished highway, a monarch butterfly landed fifteen feet in front of me—and then another, and another. Stretching down the road in front of me, living orange lamps lined my morning path. "You've answered me," I said. The monarchs flew away. I added, "And You are also laughing at me."

Judy Petsonk (born 1945) is the coauthor of *The Intermarriage Handbook* and author of *Taking Judaism Personally: Creating a Meaningful Spiritual Life,* an account of her return to Jewish religious practice through the Jewish Renewal movement.

From *Taking Judaism Personally: Creating a Meaningful Spiritual Life* (The Free Press, 1996).

The Gods Had Decreed

Isabella Leitner

After liberation from Auschwitz, Leitner and her sisters Chicha and Rachel took to the road with thousands of other displaced prisoners, struggling to shelter and feed themselves as they searched for relatives and a way to begin their lives again.

Each day, as dusk approaches, we look for deserted homes to sleep in, homes that lodged yesterday's travelers. This kind of life calls for intuition and ingenuity. We have to share, be compassionate, crowd together, grab, run before others get there. . . .

We are helpful and kind to one another. The food we have brought along keeps us well. We keep walking during daylight, settle before dark.

On the third night we find shelter in a room with two large mattresses on the floor. A middle-aged woman joins us to share our "beds." She keeps talking about her twin daughters who were separated from her by Dr. Mengele upon their arrival at Auschwitz. She insists that her daughters are alive. Her faith in their survival is like a religious fervor.

We are skeptical, but we haven't the heart to tell her otherwise. We know that Mengele's particular passion was to perform medical experiments on twins.

We prepare for bed. Rachel and I take one mattress, Chicha and the woman the other. Suddenly, a drunken soldier enters the room. He sizes up

From *Saving the Fragments: From Auschwitz to New York* by Isabella Leitner, with Irving A. Leitner (New American Library, 1985).

the situation and chooses a bedmate . . . selecting Chicha, my dark-haired sister. He quickly undresses and turns out the light.

In the dark the middle-aged woman switches places with Chicha.

In the morning the soldier realizes the deception. He smiles, dresses, and departs. On his way out he tosses a gold watch to his most recent conquest. The woman becomes part of our wandering family.

Finally, we lose her on the road, and much later we learn that she has actually, miraculously, found her twins alive in Budapest.

On our journey the woman never stopped talking about her children. She was certain the gods had decreed that somewhere another mother would give her body to a drunken soldier, as she had done, to save her daughters' virginity. We shall always remember her faith. We do not remember her name.

It Is a Death That Brings Life

Estelle Frankel

In Judaism and many other religious traditions, spiritual awakening is described as a death or mortal blow to the individual ego. It is a death, however, that also brings life: as one enters into proper alignment with the totality that is God, healing occurs. At moments of spiritual awakening, we realize we are not only who we thought we were—not just an individual consciousness or separate self who lives within the boundaries we call "I"—but also part of an ineffable unity.

Estelle Frankel (born 1953) is a psychotherapist and a teacher of Jewish mysticism in Berkeley, California, who has written often on issues related to Judaism and psychology.

From "Shavuot: Spiritual Awakening and Community Building," *Tikkun,* May/June 1997.

God's Faith, Not Mine

SHEFA GOLD

How surprising that when faith is mentioned in our morning liturgy, it is speaking of God's faith, not mine. *Raba Emunatecha!* How great is your faithfulness!

The times when I have risked to speak or cry a prayer into the abyss that stretches out before me, when I have sung out my own essence, when the spark within me has flown out into darkness with the force and heat of my longing, only then have I been met by a Presence, a Mystery.

The universe responds to my turning. Suddenly my eyes are opened to the smallest miracles. Messages are brought to me—the breeze caresses my cheek, blue overflows from the sky into the cup of my heart, my own breath arises out of nowhere as a gift of soul for me to use and transform into giving. Suddenly the world is filled with hidden meaning and this hidden-ness beckons me deeper into my own mysteries.

In the silence that follows my song, I listen as God speaks a resounding Amen (which is related to the word *emunah*). It is God's faith in my essence, my uniqueness that allows me to then know my own beauty and purpose. And so I listen intently . . . for I find my faith in the light of this response.

SHEFA GOLD (born 1954), is a leader in Aleph: Alliance for Jewish Renewal. She received her rabbinic ordination both from the Reconstructionist Rabbinical College and from Rabbi Zalman Schachter-Shalomi. Her liturgical writings and music are used by congregations across the United States.

The Grandest Mystery of All

Nina Beth Cardin

Faith is that attitude, part gift, part victory hard won, that allows each of us to look into our children's eyes, full of trust and purity, expectation and a little fear, and say to them, "I am so glad that I was able to bring you into this world." Despite all the ugliness we know that the world possesses, despite war and hatred, greed and poverty that spoil the planet and erode the spirit, despite even the inevitability of death itself, faith is what lets us say, "Dear child, it is still good." Faith is what causes us to hum absent-mindedly, and to dream about tomorrow, though tomorrow may never come. Faith may just be the grandest mystery of all. And who in this world doesn't love a mystery?

Nina Beth Cardin (born 1953), a Conservative rabbi, is editor of *Sh'ma: A Journal of Jewish Responsibility.*

An Uninterrupted Dialogue

ETTY HILLESUM

You have made me so rich, oh God, please let me share out Your beauty with open hands. My life has become an uninterrupted dialogue with You . . . one great dialogue. Sometimes when I stand in some corner of the camp, my feet planted on Your earth, my eyes raised toward Your heaven, tears sometimes run down my face, tears of deep emotion and gratitude. At night, too, when I lie in my bed and rest in You, oh, God, tears of gratitude run down my face, and that is my prayer.

HILLESUM wrote these remarks in a letter from Westerbork dated 18 August 1943, four weeks before she was sent to Auschwitz.

From *An Interrupted Life*.

God Will Raise Us Up Again

ANNE FRANK

11 April 1944

It is God that has made us as we are, but it will be God, too, who will raise us up again. If we bear all this suffering and if there are still Jews left, when it is over, then Jews, instead of being doomed, will be held up as an example. Who knows, it might even be our religion from which the world and all peoples learn good, and for that reason and that reason only do we have to suffer now. . . .

Be brave! Let us remain aware of our task and not grumble, a solution will come, God has never deserted our people; right through the ages there have been Jews, through all the ages they have had to suffer, but it has made them strong too; the weak are picked off and the strong will remain and never go under!

From *The Diary of Anne Frank: The Critical Edition,* trans. Arnold J. Pomerans and B. M. Mooyaart-Doubleday, ed. David Barnouw and Gerrold van der Stroom (Doubleday, 1989).

Source Acknowledgments

Many thanks to the authors and publishers who gave permission for their work to be included in this volume.

Selections by Kim Chernin, Marcia Falk, Estelle Frankel, Betty Friedan, Tikva Frymer-Kensky, Laura Geller, Vivian Gornick, Bonna Devora Haberman, Judith Plaskow, and Naomi Wolf appeared originally in *Tikkun* magazine, a bimonthly Jewish critique of politics, culture and society. Information and subscriptions are available from *Tikkun,* 26 Fell Street, San Francisco, CA 94102. Reprinted with permission of *Tikkun* magazine.

Selections by Rachel Adler, Riv-Ellen Prell, Alice Shalvi, and Carol Tavris appeared originally in LILITH, The Independent Jewish Women's Magazine, 250 West 57th St., New York, NY 10107. Sample copies may be requested from this address. Copyright © Lilith Publications, Inc. Reprinted with permission of the authors and *Lilith* magazine.

Selections by Amy Eilberg, Sue Levi Elwell, Minnie D. Louis, Adah Menken, Julia Richman, and Fanchon Shur were taken from *Four Centuries of Jewish Women's Spirituality: A Sourcebook,* ed. Ellen M. Umansky and Dianne Ashton (Boston: Beacon Press), 1992. The writings by Eilberg, Elwell, and Shur were reprinted with permission of their authors.

Selections by Rachel Luzzatto Morpurgo, Serel bat Jacob, Sara Coppia Sullam, and Rebecca Tiktiner are presented as published in *Written Out of History: Our Jewish*

Foremothers, ed. Sondra Henry and Emily Taitz (New York: Biblio Press), 1990. Reprinted with permission of Biblio Press.

Selections by Tova Berger, Susannah Heschel, and Susan Seidelman appeared originally in *The Invisible Thread* by Diana Bletter and Lori Grinker (Philadelphia: The Jewish Publication Society), 1989. Reprinted with permission of The Jewish Publication Society.

Selections by Nina Beth Cardin, Shoshanna Gershenzon, Shefa Gold, Sally Priesand, and Savina Teubal were written for this volume.

Agosin   "The God of Children" by Marjorie Agosin from *Zones of Pain*. Translated by Cola Franzen. Copyright 1988. Reprinted with the permission of White Pine Press, 10 Village Square, Fredonia, N.Y. 14063.

Bina   from *Words on Fire: One Woman's Journey into the Sacred* by Vanessa Ochs (New York: Harcourt Brace Jovanovich), 1990, as reprinted in "On the Path to Power: Women Decode the Talmud in Their Own Style," *Lilith,* Summer 1990. Reprinted with permission of Vanessa Ochs.

Broner   "Dayenu," from *The Women's Haggadah* by E. M. Broner with Naomi Nimrod, as published in *The Telling* (San Francisco: HarperSanFrancisco, 1993). Copyright E. M. Broner. Reprinted with permission of E. M. Broner.

Eichengreen   *From Ashes to Life: My Memories of the Holocaust* by Lucille Eichengreen (San Francisco: Mercury House, 1994). Reprinted with permission of Mercury House.

Feld   "We All Stood Together" and "Bikur Cholim" are reprinted by permission of the State University of New York Press, from *A Spiritual Life* by Merle Feld. Forthcoming, © State University of New York. All rights reserved.

Felman   "L'Dor V Dor: From Generation to Generation" by Jyl Lynn Felman in *Her Face in the Mirror: Jewish Women on Mothers and Daughters,* ed. Faye Moskowitz (Boston: Beacon Press, 1994). Reprinted with permission of the author.

Greenberg   from "A Yeshiva Girl Among the Feminists" in *On Women and Judaism* (Philadelphia: The Jewish Publication Society, 1981). Reprinted with permission of The Jewish Publication Society.

Hellerstein   "The Difference: Yom Kippur, 5745" by Kathryn Hellerstein, first published in *Bridges,* Fall 1991, vol. 2, no. 2. Copyright 1998 Kathryn Hellerstein. Reprinted with permission of the author.

Hillesum   *An Interrupted Life: The Diaries of Etty Hillesum, 1941–1943,* translated by Arno Pomerans (New York: Pantheon Books, 1983). English translation copyright © 1983 by Jonathan Cape Ltd. Copyright © 1981 by De Haan/Unibock b.v., Bussum. Reprinted with permission of Pantheon Books, a division of Random House, Inc.

Kaye/Kantrowitz   "To Be a Radical Jew in the Late 20th Century" by Melanie Kaye/Kantrowitz in *The Tribe of Dina: A Jewish Women's Anthology,* co-edited by Melanie Kaye/Kantrowitz and Irena Klepfisz (Montpelier, Vt.: Sinister Wisdom, 1986). © Melanie Kaye/Kantrowitz. Reprinted with permission of the author.

Kessler   "Covenant," first published in *Tikkun,* July/August 1989. Reprinted with permission of the author.

Klagsbrun   Untitled column in *Moment,* August 1992. Reprinted with permission of the author.

Kushner   from "Meditation Before Mikvah" by Noa Rachael Kushner, published in *Choosing a Jewish Life* by Anita Diamant (New York: Schocken Books, 1996). Reprinted with permission of the author.

Lichtenstein   "Believing Is *Seeing*," *Applied Judaism: Selected Jewish Science Essays* by Tehilla Lichtenstein (New York: Society of Jewish Science). Copyright 1989 Society of Jewish Science. ISBN 0-943745-080-X, all rights reserved. Reprinted by permission of Society of Jewish Science.

Metzger   "Eulogy for Our Mother Miryam," *CCAR Journal,* Summer 1997. Reprinted with permission of the author and *CCAR Journal.*

Moskowitz   *A Leak in the Heart* by Faye Moskowitz (Boston: David R. Godine, 1985). Copyright © 1985 by Faye Moskowitz. Reprinted with permission of Russell & Volkening as agents for the author.

Ozick   pp. 98–99, "Love Is What We Do," *Portland: The University of Portland Magazine,* Winter 1997. Reprinted with permission of the author.   p. 182, "Remember the Sabbath Day to Keep It Holy," *Self,* December 1997. Reprinted with permission of the author.

Pogrebin   "Confessions of a Contradictory Jew," *National Council of Jewish Women Journal,* Spring 1998. Reprinted with permission of the author.

Reimers   "mikveh journal" in *lechem tafayl,* the student journal of Jewish Theological Seminary, ed. David Seidenberg, vol. 1, issue 1, Winter 1990. Reprinted with permission of the author.

Rich   Excerpt from "Split at the Root: An Essay on Jewish Identity" from *Blood, Bread, and Poetry: Selected Prose 1979–1985* by Adrienne Rich (New York: W. W. Norton, 1986). Copyright © 1986 by Adrienne Rich. Reprinted by permission of the author and W. W. Norton & Company, Inc.

Rivers   from *Enter Talking* by Joan Rivers (New York: Delacorte Press, 1986). Copyright © 1986 by Joan Rivers. Reprinted with permission of Dell Books, a division of Bantam Doubleday Dell Publishing Group, Inc.

Roiphe   pp. 120–21, "What Being Jewish Means to Me" by Anne Roiphe, *The New York Times,* September 12, 1993. Reprinted from the American Jewish Committee series "What Being Jewish Means to Me," with permission of the author and the American Jewish Committee.   p. 143, *Generation Without Memory: A Jewish Journey in Christian America* by Anne Roiphe (New York: Summit Books, 1981). Reprinted with permission of the author.

Rooks   "Prayer," *CCAR Journal,* Summer 1997. Reprinted with permission of the author and *CCAR Journal*.

Roseanne   *My Life as a Woman* by Roseanne Barr (New York: Harper & Row,

Picture Acknowledgments

Page iii   Life Cycle. Julie Delton. St. Paul, MN, 1997. Ink on paper. ©Julie Delton.

Page 1   Rapture. Julie Delton. St. Paul, MN, 1994. Ink and wax on paper. ©Julie Delton.

Page 12   Husband and Wife. Amy Hill. New York, 1989. Colored pencil on paper. ©Amy Hill.

Page 21   She Blew the Shofar. Lynne Feldman. Rochester, NY, 1994. Serigraph. ©Lynne Feldman.

Page 43   Portrait of the Artist's Wife and Granddaughter. Max Lieberman. Berlin, 1926. Oil on canvas. Gift of the Jewish Cultural Reconstruction, Inc. From the collection of HUC Skirball Cultural Center and Museum. Photography by Susan Einstein.

Page 59   Tradition. Julie Delton. St. Paul. MN, 1995. Ink and wax on paper. ©Julie Delton.

Page 85   Vigil. Julie Delton. St. Paul. MN, 1996. Ink on paper. ©Julie Delton.

Page 101   Emigrants at the Railroad Station. Ida Bernstein. Los Angeles, c. 1980. Etching on paper. From the collection of HUC Skirball Cultural Center and Museum. Photography by Lelo Carter. ©Ida Bernstein.

Page 103   HaKotel. Lila Wahrhaftig. Oakland, CA, 1990. Drypoint. ©Lila Wahrhaftig.

Page 113   Passover Seder. S. Gerzowitch. Jerusalem, 1990. Pencil and watercolor on paper. From the collection of HUC Skirball Cultural Center and Museum. Photography by Lelo Carter.

Page 133   My Mother. Ida Bernstein. Los Angeles, 1976. Oil on canvas. From the collection of HUC Skirball Cultural Center and Museum. Photography by Lelo Carter. ©Ida Bernstein.

Page 145   Biala Podlaska, 1991: Even the Tombstones Were Destroyed. Yochka Lifshitz. Kibbutz Nir Oz, Israel, 1991–93. Photo montage. From the collection of the Los Angeles Museum of the Holocaust. ©Yochka Lifshitz

Page 169   Sabbath Malka II. Rose Ann Chasman. Chicago, 1989. Papercut. ©Rose Ann Chasman

Page 181   Purim Dance. Lynne Feldman. Rochester, NY. ©Lynne Feldman.

Page 195   Anne Frank. Morris Broderson. Los Angeles, c. 1972. Watercolor on paper. From the collection of HUC Skirball Cultural Center and Museum. Photography by Lelo Carter.

About the Editor

ELLEN JAFFE-GILL (born 1954) is a journalist who taught for fourteen years in the Los Angeles public schools. As Ellen Jaffe McClain, she is the author of *Embracing the Stranger: Intermarriage and the Future of the American Jewish Community* (Basic Books, 1995) and a novel for children 10–14, *No Big Deal* (Puffin, 1997). She has published numerous articles in national publications, including *Moment, Seventeen, YM, Popular Computing, New Body,* and *The Village Voice.* An accomplished mezzo-soprano, she is currently studying for the cantorate. Ellen Jaffe-Gill lives in Culver City, California, with her husband, Spencer Gill, and their Dalmatian, Molly.